Every Other Inch a Methodist

Douglas J. Cock

EPWORTH PRESS

To the memory of Leo Sanders – gratefully

© Douglas J. Cock 1987

All rights reserved. No part of this publication may be
reproduced, stored in a retrieval system, or transmitted,
in any form or by any means, electronic, mechanical,
photocopying, recording or otherwise, without the prior
permission of the publisher, Epworth Press.

Quotations from the *Methodist Recorder* appear by courtesy
of the editor.

British Library Cataloguing in Publication Data

Cock, Douglas J.
 Every other inch a Methodist.
 1. Methodist Recorder
 I. Title
 287'.05   BX8201.M/

 ISBN 0–7162–0440–1

First published in 1987
by Epworth Press
Room 195, 1 Central Buildings
Westminster, London SW1

Printed in Great Britain by
Richard Clay Ltd, Bungay, Suffolk

Contents

1	Dyed in the Wool	1
2	One Eternal Day	18
3	Conscience in Wartime	40
4	Recording Methodism	48
5	Interviews	85
6	Acts of God	93
7	Embarrassments	101
8	The Authentic Voice of Cliff	106
9	Lay of the Last Opinion	116

'What do *you* do for a living?' asked the friendly snack-bar waitress who had just served me with coffee.

'I'm a newspaper reporter on the editorial staff of the *Methodist Recorder* – a paper dealing with church matters in general and the Methodist Church in particular,' I replied.

She carefully considered this information for a few seconds. Then she said,

'What a funny sort of job.'

1 Dyed in the Wool

'I hope you're giving my son some good advice,' said my mother, entering the room.

'Good Lord, no,' replied her brother, 'I'm not the good advice sort of uncle. I'm far more likely to be teaching him some healthy rebellion.'

My teenage heart warmed to him immediately. Uncle Jack, whom I saw only on his infrequent visits from London to North Devon, was at that time an artist of considerable distinction, indeed fame, who had written several books on the art of water colour, some in conjunction with Leonard Richmond, another artist of the same school. My uncle's *Art for All* series was widely used in schools. The walls of my parents' Bideford home were heavily hung with early John Littlejohns originals, chiefly of rustic scenes. Even the most immature, done when he was young, showed sure promise of the talent to come. An outstanding feature of many of them was the versimilitude of the water, which always looked as if it would splash if you threw a stone at it.

His father, William Littlejohns, was born in Wooly, near Welcombe, where his father was a carpenter. My maternal grandfather was proud of the fact that he had been baptized, prepared for confirmation and married by the gifted and eccentric Parson Hawker, vicar of Morwenstow.

William Littlejohns, who had virtually no schooling, saved up enough money from pittances received as a carpenter's assistant to go to night school and learn to read and write with passable skill, eventually setting himself up in business as a carpenter in his own right. When I was a little boy, he would read to me, and if he came upon a difficult word always substituted for it the word 'Jerusalem', sometimes with surprising results. He wore an ear-to-ear beard, white in his latter years when I knew him, originally grown because of a skin complaint. It had the fortuitous effect of giving him a benign rustic appearance which fitted his nature. He spoke with a pronounced Devonshire accent, peppered his speech with biblical-sounding 'haths', 'doths', and 'saiths', and had a considerable gift for vivid narrative. If I showed him a new toy – tame by today's standards – he would examine it admiringly, and exclaim, 'What they will make fer money, as the woman zed when 'er zee'd the monkey.'

Thrown out of his Northam home by his landlord, he walked to the Bideford building still called York Cottage (though it is quite a sizeable house) and bought it on the spot with the sovereigns in his pocket, determined that summary dismissal from his home was a fate that would not befall him twice.

Latterly, he was looked after at York Cottage by my mother's cousin. My mother was summoned there when he was expected to die of pneumonia at the age of ninety. In the middle of the night, he sat up in bed and asked for a basin of broth 'like mother' (his late wife) 'used to make'. As the doctor had said he would probably choke if he tried to eat, his bedside watchers not surprisingly demurred, and tried to dissuade him. But William Littlejohns was a man of grim determination of the unbending kind sometimes called obstinacy, and insisted. To humour him, they prepared this delicacy in a cup, convinced he would not succeed in taking any of it – but he sat bolt upright and promptly consumed the lot. Then he repeated, 'Now bring me some in a basin like mother used to do.'

They did, he polished it off, and lived another four years, getting out and about. One day on the little lawn in front of York Cottage, he had a minor stroke. The doctor assured him and my aunt that he would nevertheless live to be a hundred. But he, frightened and not wishing to be a nuisance to anyone, asserted he had had a good life, and firmly refused to take further food or drink and, though his lips were moistened from time to time, with the same tenacity that he had recovered from pneumonia when already a nonagenarian, decided quite contentedly that he would die. And die he did, in the firm assurance that he would rejoin his wife – who had been a devout Methodist class leader and, by all accounts, a saint. I dimly remember her as a bed-ridden figure to whose presence I would be almost ceremoniously conducted.

Their children were a surprising trio to result from such a union. They represented the three arts. John trained at Bideford Art school, and gave up an art scholarship to teach painting and drawing at Westminster School, excelling in this and at lecturing and writing. He achieved great success at the Royal Academy and the Paris Salon, and (although he died in England) towards the end of his life was lionized as a portrait painter in South Africa.

As a youth, he had had a brief spell as a local preacher (though whether he ever became what Methodists call 'fully accredited' I do not know). He threw this up to embrace and propagate the cause of Socialism, until told he must either give up public speaking or his addiction to smoking. He chose the former course and on those rare occasions when he was not smoking a pipe, he was smoking either a cigarette or a cigar.

For some years he concentrated on oils, then collaborated with Leonard Richmond in writing *The Art of Painting in Pastel*, followed a few years later by *The Technique of Water-Colour*. He exhibited in the USA, and at home in many London galleries as well as at Swansea, Hereford, Harrogate and Bristol, notably at the latter his colourful 'Flower Garden at Nice'. He was a successful book illustrator, and sales of his books reached over a quarter of a million. He wrote for educational papers, lectured all over the country, and became a member of the Royal Institute of Painters in Water Colours, Royal Society of British Artists, Royal Society of Painters in Water Colours and the Pastel Society. He designed about a dozen posters for the old LNER.

He usually wore a bow tie, and in his younger days exhibited a certain bohemianism when he fell among the Chelsea set. I recall him as an upright, dapper man, his neat moustache tinged with nicotene. When I knew him he had long since abandoned the faith of his fathers and he took an impish delight in utterances deliberately designed to wound the susceptibilities of the faithful. This was fairly easy to do in the restricted, rustic Victorian world in which he grew up. His ideas greatly shocked his saintly, fundamentalist mother. To the end of his days, he remained an agreeable, cultured reprobate. Like the Undershaft of Shaw's *Major Barbara*, he did not so much *do* immoral things as say and think them. It was this which in the play so disturbed Lady Britomart, who could not forgive her husband for preaching immorality while he practised morality.

My uncle once told me that someone had been loud in praise of the previous night's sunset and added, 'That gave him away at once. It showed the man had no sense of colour at all. That sunset was the most hideous clash of colours you could possibly imagine.'

His sister Annie was a freelance writer, chiefly contributing to regional periodicals. She also taught typewriting. She wrote several plays, some of which were produced in the north of England, and dialect stories, some of which appeared in the *Bristol Times and Mirror*. She also wrote operattas for the opening of bazaars at Bideford's Bridge Street Methodist Church. She was a more or less permanent invalid, usually described as 'delicate'. The word suited her in other senses than the medical one. There was about her slight frame something of the fragility of Dresden china. There were times when she seemed to belong to another age, a pale ghost from the early Victorian era. Yet many of her writings showed signs of a desire to embrace what in those days passed for modernism. Some of her shorter pieces would be about flappers who said 'ripping', charlestoned and sported Eton crops. None of this really suited her. She had greater affinity with the world of James Barrie, Walter de la Mare and A. A. Milne. When not in bed, she sat with a woollen shawl round her shoulders, often close to the fire, near a small table crammed with medicine bottles in a room smelling like a hospital ward. She was not, I think, a hypochondriac; yet latterly when she ventured out, at the least suggestion of an east wind she would gently retrace her steps. She was an avid experimenter with anything in the nature of alternative medicine. She died in 1927 aged forty-nine. I was twelve. Her father, still going strong, was eighty-seven.

She weaned me from the comics of my boyhood to a more satisfying literature. Like many little boys of those days, I took *The Rainbow*. It was not only the adventures of the Bruin Boys and Tiger Tim to which I looked forward on Thursdays – but also to a picture-serial of a brother and sister who wandered into the woods and there were captured by gipsies who treated them cruelly – intended, I think, as a warning to the paper's young readers not to 'play with the gipsies in the wood'. Had I in those childish days a sado-masochistic streak? I know I eagerly looked forward to the pictures which showed the evil pair (a man and wife) taking the children roughly into their old-fashioned caravan to beat them soundly with a broom.

It was my aunt who introduced me to the lovable lunacy of Lewis Carrol's *Alice* and the deep understanding of the child mind of Kenneth Grahame's *Dream Days*. She encouraged me to write; and it was probably because of her influence that I went in for journalism. At all events, the Saturday visits to York Cottage were more exciting than *The Perils of Pauline* had been.

I went to York Cottage on Saturdays for tea with my aunt and grandfather, after watching silent films from the 'fourpennies' at the Palace Cinema. Those were the days of Felix the Cat cartoons, Tom Mix and Chaplin two-reelers over which men of my generation are boringly nostalgic. I recall the cinema manager as a tall and aristocratic man, wearing plus-fours, who from time to time would stalk down to the front of the screen and deliver a brief lecture concerning our behaviour. 'I don't mind your clapping,' he would tell us, 'but I will not stand all that hissing, booing and stamping of feet.' Then, as he returned to the back of the cinema, we took advantage of his explicit permission by according him a thunderous round of applause. Once, when a Rudolf Valentino film was showing soon after the star's death, he solemnly pointed out that his immortality was assured 'through the miracle of the cinema', and appealed to us to behave with fitting decorum. Usually an unruly mob, this reference to death touched a sensitive nerve and we duly complied.

The other child, Florence, my mother, was a professional singer and music teacher before her marriage. In my boyhood, before radios (or, as we called them, wireless sets) were necessities rather than luxuries, the low wall in front of my parents' bungalow would on many evenings be packed with listeners to the rehearsals of the chorus work which took place in the front room for the local productions of Gilbert and Sullivan operas.

My paternal grandfather was a typical Nonconformist of the period – short, upright, neatly bearded, an alderman, twice Bideford's Mayor, a builder by trade (my father and one of his brothers carried on the business), a staunch teetotaller and a radical Liberal. Most of all, he was a Methodist, active in the offices of the church he helped, both in the physical and the spiritual sense, to build. For Bideford's Bridge Street Wesleyan Church was built by the (then) firm of Lamerton and Cock – or, as our family preferred to call it, Cock and Lamerton.

This was the church which was to achieve notoriety by nearly becoming the subject of a High Court case. Much River Torridge water has passed under Bideford's many-arched bridge since then. I certainly never dreamt the day would come when I would travel to London in order to hear the case (arising out of the desire of a minority of the trustees to reverse the decision to close it) officially dropped when, in legal jargon, it was 'mentioned' to Mr Justice Plowman in the Chancery Division of the High Court. He, having heard the terms by which all parties (including the Attorney General) agreed that litigation should cease, gave his formal assent and approved them.

This was one of the most troublesome disagreements of

many that arose out of the fusion of an ex-Wesleyan and ex-United Methodist church in one town. 'Redundancy' was a thorny problem which existed much more pressingly in many a village than ever it did in Bideford and continued to cause conflict long after the Methodist Union of 1932.

What determined the whole future course of my life was a simple piece of ecclesiastical administration. Rev. Leo Sanders was appointed to be the minister of Bridge Street Wesleyan Church.

'Methodist valuations' Dr Rattenbury once wrote 'are difficult sometimes even for a Methodist to understand; most intelligent outsiders, as the editor of a famous journal once told me, give them up in despair!'

Even allowing for the fact that I met Leo at the impressionable age of seventeen, I still marvel at his relative connexional obscurity in view of the notoriety of much lesser men. No man is strong, it has been said, unless he bears within his character antitheses strongly marked. Leo balanced almost perfectly a deep spirituality with a down-to-earth practicality, a gentleness, patience and winsomeness with a certain rugged masculinity. Not until after his death did I come to realize that in life he had carried about him a certain indefinable aura.

At the age of seventeen, he had volunteered as a stretcher-bearer in the first world war, and saw the bitterest fighting of its trench warfare. One day a shell dropped right beside him, killing all his comrades and leaving him wounded in the back, with shrapnel wounds in the head as well. This affected him for the rest of his life – and he once said that never since then had he known what it was not to have a headache. But not for many years did he discover that he had sustained a fractured spine.

From Penryn near Falmouth, where he ministered briefly during the second world war, he became a Royal Air Force chaplain. When he reported for his medical, he left the splints he then had to wear in the hotel, and three days later returned to Cornwall wearing a chaplain's uniform. His subsequent ministry was a distinguished and fruitful one for which his temperament, utter dedication and all his experiences had signally equipped him. He gave himself without reserve and (as always) beyond the limits of his strength, to men's needs at South Cerney. In 1944 he was awarded the MBE for 'raising the general morale of the station'. He was the first on the scene after a Lancaster bomber crashed, and took charge of the rescue operations. He served in India and Germany, Dishforth, Cosford and Halton, and was appointed Assistant Principal Chaplain.

This lay in the future when, in the early thirties, he came to Bideford, still a fairly quiet market town. The first world war was only fourteen years away, and his first reputation was that of a sort of Woodbine Willie. His memories of Flanders were still vivid and provided him with stunning and sometimes searing sermon illustrations. His deep social conscience, virile personality and intensely sincere preaching made an instant impact, indeed something of a sensation, during those inter-war days of depression.

One day, an Oxford Group team, led by A. J. Russell, author of the best-selling book *For Sinners Only*, came to Bideford. Leo volunteered to chauffeur them around. Doing so, he spoke frankly about some of the frustrations of his work and his dissatisfactions with what he was increasingly finding to be the unacceptable face of institutional Christianity. In characteristic fashion, they turned the tables and said, 'What are *you* doing about it?' The outcome was an enrichment of his Christian experience; and he soon became the natural leader of a growing local group.

I had just left school – Queen's College, Taunton, a Methodist foundation – and was putting into sometimes frantic practice my newly acquired Pitman's Shorthand on Richard Acland's espousal of 'Collective Security' as he canvassed the North Devon constituency prior to the General Election in which he won the seat for the Liberals. He founded the short-lived Commonwealth Party, later becoming a Labour MP, only commendably to resign on a point of principle (Labour's refusal to abandon the H-Bomb) and so cut short what promised to be a distinguished parliamentary career. I now meet him occasionally at Sunday morning meetings of Exeter's Society of Friends which (while remaining a Methodist) I frequently attend.

Leo had just started a men's meeting, and was asking people not skilled in public speaking to talk on 'Old Age and Christianity', 'The Working Man and Christianity' and the like. He asked me to speak on 'Youth and Christianity'.

I accepted with alacrity, went along and declaimed,

If Christ had been a weakling, I should never have accepted his doctrine. Christ professed to ignore all creeds. He certainly rejected all previous ones, but he equally certainly put a new one in their place. A better one, I admit, but still a creed. But even if it had been an infinitely worse one, it would have been all the same to me. Christ has convinced me that Christianity is the only hope for this world; but a man with his personality would convince me that absolute rejection of Christianity was the only hope for this world. Perhaps it is a good thing that no man, Christian or heretic, has ever had the personality of our Lord. Because, don't you see, a man's personality is all we care for, all that's worth caring for, and all we ever shall care for, unless we are very, very careful, unless we refuse to allow experience to make us grow up, become disillusioned and thoroughly uninteresting. Of course it's unreasonable. But Reason has failed us so many times, our Instinct never.

I ended, to a slightly bemused men's meeting:

There's only one thing for them (i.e. youth) to do, and that is just what they feel like doing, whether it's logical or not. And if they're good at heart – and most of them are – they won't go far wrong if they obey their instincts. But I DO wish to goodness they'd stop listening to what their elders tell them, and go their own way. They are by far the best judges of what they ought to do. They know what they want to do, and *that* is what they ought to do.

Thanking me, Leo Sanders (to whom I was a complete stranger) said he sometimes thought that what youth most needed was a thundering good hiding. But some weeks later, I knelt down in his manse, and in the language of the Oxford Group, my life was changed, or in my grandfather's language, I was converted. I walked down Bideford's High Street looking very serious and clutching the copy of *For Sinners Only* Leo had lent me, where a picture was taken by a street photographer. Ever vain, a few days later I collected the postcard print of myself taken when, spiritually speaking, I was only a few minutes old.

More dramatic than my adolescent experience was the case of Beverley Cotton. Leo Sanders first met him in the vagrants' ward of a local hospital where he introduced himself by saying, 'I bet I know where those gauntlet gloves you're wearing came from.' He turned out to be right, and Leo gave him an invitation card to his Men's Own.

One evening when that meeting was in full swing, the caretaker came in, in a highly explosive state. 'There's a man outside with one of your cards,' he said.

'Then show him in,' said Leo.

'He's roaring drunk.'

'Then put him in the minister's vestry.'

There until the meeting ended stayed Beverley and, keeping an eye on him, the town's harbour master. At the close, Beverley, only slightly more sober, was brought into the schoolroom to play the piano, which he did by ear in true pub style, and accompanied the singing of 'Abide with me'.

His full name was Albert Henry Cotton, and his nickname of Beverley derived from his drunken attempt that night to pronounce his Christian names. He was a colourful, lovable character (when sober) and, with his bubonic nose, exaggerated air of courtliness and in the trilby hat my father gave him, reminded me of Mr Micawber as portrayed by W. C. Fields.

He was born in Birmingham, and went to Worcester when still young. His father lived at Maddisfield Court where he was estate agent for Lord Beauchamp. Beverley went to the National School and had lessons (so he told me) at the same school as Edward Elgar. There began the piano playing which proved to be his undoing. Asked to give a pianoforte selection at a smoking concert at twelve years of age, he was later engaged to perform every night of the week, became a member of the local Liberal Club, and played every Sunday morning at a smoking concert for nearly four years.

His mother apprenticed him as a glove cutter, and he learnt the trade at which he became a craftsman, but through heavy drinking soon found that no one would give him work. He walked to Yeovil, where he got work and earned so much that he only worked half the week. He worked for a time at Tintunell, leaving (as he put it) 'through drink', and was given £2 to find lodgings at Martock in Somerset. Two months later he was on the road again, stopping at Yeovil.

One Sunday he went by wagonette to Sherborne, got drunk, and while walking through a churchyard to get to lodgings at Kingston slipped on a gravestone. He went to sleep there, was found by a policeman at four o'clock in the morning, and was subsequently fined half-a-crown. Too ashamed to go to his place of work, he walked to Westbury. Then he walked to Worcester, Ledbury, Abergavenny, Pontypool, Treherbert, the Rhondda, Maesteg, Bridgend, Neath, Port Talbot, Porth Cawl – and again to Worcester.

His mother and his home were gone. In four months he spent the money and property which had been left to him. Then his journeys took him to Shepton Mallett, Wells, Glastonbury, Stoke-under-Ham, Sherborne, Milburn Port, Yeovil, Chard, Bridport, Lyme Regis, Axminster, Exeter, Torrington, and finally Bideford. He earned some sort of living by playing the piano in pubs.

For a long time Beverley, under Leo's influence, lived the life of a changed man, never touching a drop. But from Bolton (where Leo was later stationed and I was living in the manse unsuccessfully candidating for the Methodist ministry) word came that Beverley had had a relapse and was, if anything, more of a drunkard than ever. He would be described as an alcoholic today. Then came the news that he was coming to Bolton, and the time of his train's arrival.

That evening, Leo came in the front door, and saying, 'Put

this in a corner,' handed me a long medieval sword wrapped in brown paper. Beverley, followed by Leo's wife and young daughter, came in and sang, danced around the table, and acted like a Victorian music-hall comedian. Next morning, he awoke full of bitter recriminations and high resolve. The sword had been found during demolition in the walls of a glove factory at Bideford. Beverley had travelled with this by train from Devon to Lancashire, in a state of high intoxication.

From then on, he lived on a moral see-saw. For weeks he would be utterly dependable and once, when the others went down with 'flu, took complete charge of household duties, including cooking the meals. Then he would disappear, perhaps for a day only (in which case he might return late at night in a condition ranging from tipsy to paralytic) or for weeks or months. Once a phone call came from a Manchester hotel asking for someone to meet him with a car. Instead, a friend went there by train, and succeeded in getting him from one of that city's stations to the other only by granting his every whim, that is, going into every pub en route.

When he was in repentant mood I would drive him around Manchester seeking glove cutting work which he would carry out in a shed at the rear of the manse to pay off his drinking debts. Once I did this in a pea-souper of a fog, Beverley leaning out of the window and guiding me with, 'In a bit, Doug, out a bit, Doug.' Once I got out of the car to ascertain whether I was in the road or on the pavement, to find that the bonnet of the car was tight against the window of Lewis's shop front.

At that moment I was supposed to be on stage in an operetta which the church (St Helen's Road Methodist Church, Bolton) was putting on. I was understudied in the first act in my part of a town crier, and received a round of applause upon my late entrance. The operetta was *Dogs of Devon* and I was always distinctly amused to hear the chorus singing, 'Bang the droom, Drake's droom.'

I was conscious of having inherited in the movement to which I belonged a richer appropriation and a more committed expression of faith than anything I had found in 'organized Christianity' – a phrase always employed in a derogatory sense. We had the intoxicating sense of being the possessors, if not of a new truth, at any rate of a superior manifestation of the faith once delivered to the saints. I still incline to believe that there was some measure of truth in that conception. To use a word much in vogue today, it was a more 'relevant' expression of Christianity than any I have encountered since.

It was and remains unique in the field of Christian propaganda and permeation. I insist upon the 'Christian' as Dr Buchman would have done, and did. The two names by which the movement was known – the Oxford Group and Moral Re-Armament – were both inadequate, if not misleading. It was never merely humanist. 'You will never, never, never come into this experience until you know the Cross of Christ,' Frank unequivocally declared. On the other hand, it was not (as some critics asserted or implied) what is generally understood by revivalist. 'Revival is only one level of thought,' said Frank. 'To stop there is inferior thinking. The next step is revolution . . . There is a third stage – renaissance.'

But my reluctance to become part of Methodism, or a sense of having been sent to bring into it something profound and far-reaching, I was beginning to recognize as a subtle form of spiritual pride. I was also beginning to realize the truth of T. S. Eliot's insight that if the Temple is to be cast down, it must first be built.

There were certain characteristic Oxford Group phenomena. With its genius for adapting current fashion and usage to its own purpose, the Oxford Group first held house parties. Later, as war clouds lowered, these were superseded by Moral Re-Armament assemblies, lending support to the ill-informed charge that MRA was Fascist both in organization and sympathy. I have been to many Christian gatherings (mostly Methodist) since those days but none to equal the disciplined and frequently uncomfortable quality of that unique fellowship with its insistence on 'guided strategy'.

They were heady days, and there was much to be excited about. Lives were being changed, men and women untouched by the ministrations of what I sometimes contemptuously dismissed as 'organized religion' were swelling this rising tide, the thing was growing, solving social and to some extent international problems, and assuming the proportions of a national movement.

They were also the years when a second world war seemed daily more likely. The Korda–H. G. Wells film *Things to Come* was scaring everybody. MRA presented a new hope and way of escape. I thrilled to the music of young George Fraser, a little Edinburgh song writer and former cinema organist from the days of silent films, though I did not then recognize the strong Wagnerian influence in his music. He also wrote the words and music of 'Wise Old Horsey', a catchy little number with an effective rhythm, sung in the film *Youth Marches On* by handsome, six-foot-five Cecil Broadhurst, who sang cowboy songs on Canadian radio to his own ukulele accompaniment. This unique short film told the story of 200 young men, who had met for ten days in June 1937, in a camp on the Canadian prairies. Some had travelled over 2,000 miles and made a considerable sacrifice to share in the camp. Their declared, idealistic aim was to train physically and spiritually for their countries' rebuilding.

'We're making Empire history,' George Fraser had said. 'It must be filmed and shown to the world. It will stir youth in every country.' He talked it over with the others, who all agreed. They had no technical equipment, little experience, and between them £35 in their pockets. One sold a pair of binoculars, one a life insurance policy – and thus the film was financed.

The film profiled three young men, from very different backgrounds, during their time at the camp, watched their reactions, and finally showed how 'all enlisted in a growing army of New Frontiersmen to bring God's plan to their countries'. Cecil Broadhurst was ideally cast as the singing cowboy, Paul Campbell and Ted Devlin as a truck driver and a student. There was no time to work out a detailed script, so as they went along they shot the scenes they thought they would need. When twenty-five of the campers were commissioned by the Premier of Saskatchewan to take their message to England, their cameraman – a chemist and old-time Hollywood cameraman from silent film days – came too. Just before starting, George Fraser cabled to producer Eric Parfitt in London, 'Arriving with 3,000 feet of film.' That June, the film was showing at five West End cinemas in the same week. There were 300 bookings in two months. 'I seem to be wrong about this film,' said the head of a large circuit, who had turned it down.

In September 1938, I went to Interlaken, a little Swiss chalet town set in a deep hollow between two ridges of mountains. There, in the shadow of the Jungfrau, I was one of about 2,000 representatives of over forty nations at a Moral Re-Armament assembly.

The big English contingent came in two specially chartered cross-channel boats and express trains labelled 'Oxfordgruppe'. We arrived late on the Friday night, and were met by a cheering crowd of those already at Interlaken. Every omnibus in the town was booked that night to take the English to their hotels. Special arc lights had to be installed at the station to help disperse the huge crowd. All the English arrivals were helped by Scottish boys in kilts, standing by with luggage trollies, looking bright, clean and efficient. I spent that first night in a primitive and essentially Swiss youth hostel. When I woke, I saw the Jungfrau and the town for the first time. I washed and shaved, bare from the waist up, in the clear, fresh open air. Later, parties arrived from Greece, Kenya, Bulgaria, Latvia, Sweden, Norway, Denmark, Finland, Holland, Germany, France, Palestine, and other countries.

A major European crisis was developing, there was tension in the air. The assembly's declared aim was 'to create entirely new and friendly relations between countries of rival ideologies, to replace hatred with understanding, and jealousy with co-operation'.

Dr Buchman asked in one of his speeches:

What is the answer to this negative cloud that hangs over the whole of Europe? What will drive away the clouds that have been hanging over the Jungfrau during these ominous days? The very mountains seem to reflect the mood of a disturbed Europe. We must bridge seemingly impossible and humanly hopeless situations. We need to reach a whole new level of thinking, willing and living. The Oxford Group's aim ever since the last war has been to give a whole new pattern for statesmanship and a whole new level of responsible thinking. These faculties are only given to men who are living under God's guidance. Our aim is to make the world as different positively as war could make it negatively. The aim and answers of Interlaken remain the one basic necessity for every nation, the only permanent answer for war and the only adequate foundation for reconciliation, reconstruction and lasting peace.

Whole families came with their children, so many that there was a nursery hotel where they played games and started each day with a 'quiet time', all listening for God's guidance with the same seriousness as their parents. At ease in their company was Tod Sloan, a gnarled and grizzled former left-wing agitator. 'I have been in another revolution for forty-seven years,' he said. 'I fought against the system that made bombs and guns, hunger and unemployment. Now I am in this revolution with all of you, because it brings all nations and classes together to build a new world.'

There was small, frail, grey-haired and determined Mrs Jaegar, whose family had sold their little shop in a north-country industrial English town for £30 to make the journey possible. (Dr Buchman said, 'This family do not crave your sympathy. God is their security.') There was something almost frighteningly simple in the way this little old lady quietly rose at one of the large assemblies, and said of her arrival in a foreign country: 'When I got there, I found that so many had not seen beyond their own personal salvation. I had to go and see a Member of Parliament, and as I only spoke English, I took an interpreter. We talked for an hour and a half, and the MP's life was changed.'

The main hall of the Kursall just held the 2,000 people there. On the last Sunday morning, those outside fetched ladders and climbed up the narrow balcony where they clung precariously to the window sills. It was then that, during the whole assembly's only collection, men going round with baskets had great difficulty in getting through the dense crowd, so they passed the baskets up the lines while they stood in the middle. One collector's face was a study when he saw his basket disappearing out of the window to be handed to those clinging to the ledges.

Two thousand people were present, representing over forty nations. There were company directors, manual workers, unemployed people, MPs, sportsmen, bishops, youth of forty nations, naval and military men, heads of big business. All parts of the then British Empire were represented, as well as the Oslo States, the Little Entente, the Balkan States, the USA, China, Japan, France and Germany. A film and radio star and a peer, a Trade Union leader and the head of a big business combine found themselves side by side. A Bulgarian who since childhood had devoted himself to the work of the Macedonian revolutionary movement and stirring up hatred against Bulgarian neighbours, the Greeks and Yugoslavs, was on friendly terms with a Greek, his energies devoted to bringing about Balkan unity.

We left Interlaken by train one glorious morning when the sun was just rising and the haze over the waters had not yet lifted. The night we arrived we had seen nothing of the Swiss scenery, but as we left we saw the lakes and mountains receding as the train, in which we spent a whole day, sped on.

We returned to a crisis-conscious England. A year later, all Europe was at war.

2 One Eternal Day

'Damn!' said the editor of the *Methodist Recorder*, opening his copy of the *Methodist Times*, 'they've got Weatherhead.'

This was Frederick Daniel Wiseman, known as Fritz, son of Rev. Dr Frederick Luke Wiseman and grandson of Rev. Luke H. Wiseman, one of the *Methodist Recorder*'s founders. Between the wars, passengers on the top deck of buses in London's Fleet Street would sometimes glimpse at the top window of 161 the striking features of an aristocratic looking gentleman with fair hair and long sideburns (many years before this became a twentieth-century fashion), busy at his desk, smoking a cigarette in a long holder. (The *Methodist Recorder* later transferred to 116 and then to 176 – before moving away from Fleet Street in 1983 to premises in Golden Lane.)

That Thursday as I stood nervously by his desk, he had just discovered that the rival paper had enlisted the skills of Dr Leslie Weatherhead to answer readers' psychological, personal and spiritual problems.

F. D. Wiseman had originally intended to enter the medical profession. But he enlisted at the beginning of the first world war in 1914 and joined the *Recorder* staff in 1923. Unlike his successors, he never went to the annual Methodist Conference, his features were not connexionally familiar, he was almost completely the traditional anonymous editor, and not until his premature death in 1953 was his authorship of the 'Notes of the Week', which was widely read far outside church circles, generally known.

In spite of his love of Methodism's traditions, especially its hymnody, he was something of a rebel. It was partly his dissatisfaction with institutional Christianity which led him, under the influence of Rev. Cecil Rose, to identify himself with the Oxford Group.

He was essentially a shy man yet he served on county and city councils in Hertfordshire, and was a magistrate, in which capacity his judgments were invaluable, especially in juvenile courts. He had a natural rapport with youth.

I lived then in digs, next door to Dr Wiseman's house in Wandsworth Common. It was bombed during the second world war and it was later reliably reported that he was dug out from the rubble, although the additional detail that when his rescuers reached him he was singing 'O for a thousand tongues to sing my great Redeemer's praise' is generally thought to be apocryphal.

In those pre-war years, Dr Wiseman occasionally wrote 'leaders', and I would collect these from his house. They were handed to me by his housekeeper, and I never saw him. One Sunday, my landlady – a faithful and pious Baptist – went to a neighbouring Methodist Church to hear Dr Wiseman preach for the first time. She came back clearly unenthusiastic. When I pressed her, she said she had lived next door to Dr Wiseman for several years, had caught glimpses of him in his garden, and he had never once spoken to her. His text that morning had been 'Who is my neighbour?' I think an innate reticence sometimes gave him the unfair reputation of autocracy. Like his two sons, he was a great lover of people.

In those days, the *Methodist Times* represented the Methodist Church's left wing and was the organ of the Forward Movement in the time of Hugh Price Hughes. The *Recorder* was the right-wing, conservative, Establishment paper. This reputation took a little time to live down, even after fusion with the *Methodist Times* when that closed towards the end of the 1930s.

From that paper came R. G. Burnett, who succeeded Wiseman as editor in 1953, and who after *his* untimely death in 1960 was succeeded by Eric Pigott. Both these men inherited and expanded Wiseman's plans for a Christian paper which would not allow piety to be an excuse for lack of expertise. By the time *Who's Who in the Free Churches* was published in 1951, it was possible for the entry under *Methodist Recorder* (almost certainly in Wiseman's wording) to read:

> The Methodist Newspaper Co Ltd; 116 Fleet Street, London, EC4; Central 4748; *Methodist Recorder*, London; F. D. Wiseman; Weekly; 3d; Methodist. A pioneer in religious journalism in the sense that it is, in organization, a miniature counterpart of a national newspaper. The only church newspaper to give a large proportion of its space to news pictures, it has news offices in the north of England, the Midlands and the West Country, and, at one time, published special editions for Scotland, the north of England, in addition to a general edition. It carries a monthly supplement *Young Britain* which is a youth newspaper on its own. It also has a travellers' service which is ready to do anything from advising what plays to see, to arranging trips to places of national or sectional interest for Methodist visitors from overseas.

Richard Burnett was a cultured, friendly West Countryman, who one year was President of the Local Preachers' Mutual Aid Association, the official history of which, *A Goodly Fellowship*, he wrote in collaboration with F. H. Buss. During his editorship, the paper acquired a distinctive literary flavour, with more book reviews than it had had previously, and contained some of his own finely phrased and perceptive writing.

Eric Pigott, a minister's son, came as a young but already skilled newspaperman, and I was to serve under him for a much longer period than I had done under either of his immediate predecessors. A dedicated journalist (and Christian), he was keenly aware that even on a religious paper, perhaps especially on a religious paper, piety was no substitute for professional skills. He was a large man in every way – large in build, large in vision and in his concepts for the paper and the world-wide church. He was also large in his generosity.

I recall him in a happy mood walking through Preston one evening during the week when the Methodist Conference was being held there, passing a poster outside a church advertising one of the Conference's more estoric public meetings ('Methodism and the Arts', or something of the sort) and exclaiming with a great shout of laughter 'That'll empty all the pubs before closing time!' He was one of the original Westminster Laymen, which was a sort of ginger-group which aimed to reawaken the Methodist Church's sleeping conscience.

I had a warm affection and respect for Eric Pigott and Richard Burnett, and also for Michael Taylor, under whom I was also proud to serve (for a very short period), and was glad to number all of them among my friends. But Frederick Daniel Wiseman I loved.

In those early days with Wiseman in Fleet Street, in about 1935, I was mainly occupied with sub-editing copy. This included working on the regular contributions of 'Romany', Rev. G. Bramwell Evans, which were written in his own none-too-legible hand and then corrected by his wife. There was no time to type out each article, which would have been the ideal solution, but my task was somehow to make the 'copy' readable for the printers.

This short period was really a false start, led nowhere (at any rate immediately) and I returned for a time to provincial journalism. Then (more or less out of the blue) I was invited to share with circulation manager Reuben Rees, a well known *Recorder* character, the opening of the paper's northern regional office in Manchester. Rees and I would pay eighteen pence for a three-course lunch and coffee, and would refuse to patronize the few restaurants which had the effrontery to charge an extra fourpence for the coffee.

This was an experiment which only partially succeeded. Each week the regional edition carried a 'Lancashire News Page', parts of which were peculiar to itself. Sometimes prominent Methodist laymen from Lancashire, in London for a week or more, would buy a copy of the general edition. After returning home, comparison of the two editions would cause them to write to the editor complaining that they were much more interested in those wider connexional reports which had been truncated to accommodate a full-column account of some domestic happening in a northern village chapel. Still the experiment was not a complete failure and had there been no second world war it would have been extended to other regions.

The 'Lancashire News Page', in those more expansive days, was headed with pictures by W. E. Tattersall who, with his camera was, like Reuben Rees, a familiar figure at the annual Methodist Conference. I remember such captions as: 'A View of the River Wyre at Garstang', 'A group of horses in pasture at Silversdale, near Carnforth', 'Furness Abbey, Lancashire', 'The ancient sundial at Lancaster Castle'. A typical example of his style was a country background for two farm folk looking at each other, with the caption 'Lancashire workers by their home at Hochton Bottom, near Preston – Miss Yates and her father, Mr H. Yates, both staunch Methodists'.

It was the late thirties, and a common sight was a small group of men standing idly on a street corner. The 'Lancashire News Page' sometimes carried pictures of soup distribution to unemployed men of all ages. 'Soup distribution at the Blackburn Mission' one was captioned and my report read:

> A weekly distribution of soup to people in need is one of the innovations of the Blackburn Mission, for which Rev. B. Hughes Smith has been responsible. Each Thursday at noon a queue of hungry men can be seen inside the Mission awaiting their meal. The scheme was inaugurated on 1 December last year (1938) and, with the exception of Christmas week, has been maintained ever since. About 880 people have taken advantage of the 'dinner for a penny' as it has come to be known. For that sum, a meal of bread and soup can be secured. A shilling a day is the meagre sum on which many of them live.

There were no smiles on their faces – just expressions of vacant acceptance of the charity and numbed hopelessness of any sort of different future

Wigan Mission's thirty-fourth anniversary in March 1939 took place during a time of acute international tension and great industrial depression ... Wigan was once the centre of the coal trade, but the coal pits have closed one by one, leaving 6,000 miners unemployed. The rolling mills have gone, and the great iron and steel works are silent and still. Most of the mills are on short time, so that wages are correspondingly low. Unemployment, says the superintendent of the Mission, Rev. Percy S. Watkinson, has become a settled 'occupation', for many believe they will never work again. The only work that thousands in the district have done for nearly nine years was during the September crisis, when their services were utilized in digging trenches.

Nothing seemed to dampen the spirits of the Methodists of those times. They packed into Central Halls to listen to addresses by such giants as Luke Wiseman, Townley Lord, William Sangster, Donald Soper and Dr S. W. Hughes, a Baptist leader whose eloquence, compounded of sentences and parentheses of tortuous length held an inexplicable attraction for the hordes of middle aged and elderly women of the type that patronize our chapels' Women's Own afternoon meetings. They came in their thousands to sit, mesmerized, at the feet of this wizard of words, many of which they could not possibly have understood.

I recorded it all with a careful detail that would horrify any editor today. I employed tired, stock phrases. These practitioners of the platform were 'stirring', 'inspiring', 'effective', 'characteristic'. Dr Hughes was 'typical'. Sangster was 'inimitable' (an adjective in later years disproved by scores of Methodist Mike Yarwoods). Soper was 'challenging' or 'provocative'.

There were speakers of those pre-war and early post-war years whose names I have now come to revere because of later reading, and whom I should now esteem it an honour to meet and hear but who I treated then with a cursoriness bordering on contempt. Methodism's great triumvirate – Sangster, Weatherhead and Soper – I had of course admired and loved from the outset.

Shortly before the outbreak of the second world war, I called on the young Neville Ward, whose books now mean so much to me, and who then gently chided me when I told him of a story I was engaged on concerning a breakaway group at Jumbo Methodist Church, Middleton. Did I not see my task, he asked, as one of strengthening the church, or was it merely to get a good story, however damaging to the church's reputation? I reported:

> It was here that early pioneers founded the wholesale side of the Co-operative Movement.

James S. Stewart, another writer whose books always speak to my condition, I should now count it an immense privilege to hear preach. When he was one of a platform of speakers at the mission anniversary in early February 1940, at Oxford Place, Leeds (where I opened a *Methodist Recorder* office after the war, before doing the same at Exeter) he made no special appeal. In those fulsome days, I gave him short shrift.

> The Rev. James S. Stewart BD gave a forceful address on youth's search for reality, adventure and God, showing how these could only be attained through Jesus Christ.

A fair enough summary, I dare say.

I saw myself as a young, modern newspaperman, bringing fresh, realistic reporting into religious journalism. Blissful in my ignorance, my expendable phrases and clichés abounded.

> A few words appropriate to the occasion ...
>
> It was fitting that ...
>
> Two important resolutions have recently been passed by the Temperance and Social Welfare Committee (North Lancashire District). The first, moved by Rev. Harold Thompson, of Blackburn, was to the effect ...

'Was to the effect'? Oh dear.

The resolution actually read: 'that this District Temperance and Social Welfare Committee agrees to support the cotton trade's appeal to the Government in any way open to us, and we further ask the Synod to inform the Government of our determined support of their appeal for the cotton trade's fullest restoration. We also ask the Government to encourage the placing of new industries in the depressed areas of Lancashire.' It was carried unanimously.

Harold Thompson was the first minister I called on as a *Methodist Recorder* staff reporter. He was the first of a long, long line. (One December day in 1938, Reuben Rees and I went to Rochdale, and I called on twelve.) Harold Thompson gave me my first story for the paper's new venture, and I blew it up out of all proportion to its real significance. He was an outstanding minister with the sort of genius that borders on eccentricity, one of Methodism's great mission figures, with a large-hearted social concern. *Who's Who in Methodism 1933* (a *Methodist Times* publication) gave his special interests as 'wild game hunting and Arctic exploring'.

The Manchester *Recorder* office was opened at a period of serious decline for the cotton trade. When Harold Thompson, then a member of the Harwood Street branch of the Queen's Hall, Blackburn, learnt that the Prime Minister was visiting the town, he was determined that Neville Chamberlain should not leave

> without being impressed with the determination of the Lancashire people to end a long-standing grievance.

At the Queen's Hall anniversary in November 1938, he told the crowd,

> We, as a Methodist Church, say to the cotton trade that our church is behind you in any reasonable demands you make upon the Government.

In Blackburn, there were 15,503 unemployed out of an industrial field of 51,040. Three in ten were on some kind of relief.

Mr Chamberlain did not agree to meet a deputation, but

later Harold Thompson expressed himself encouraged at what the Premier had said in reply,

> although he made no reference to the part the churches might play.

Mr Thompson, who before entering the ministry had been a half-timer in a mill at Rishton, near Blackburn, said:

> I am not foolishly claiming that the Lancashire cotton trade can or ought to regain the old-time volume. On the other hand, the Prime Minister said he saw no reason why much of the trade should not be regained. Markets are not static, and millions of idle people in rags today await the service of Lancashire looms for things they can make and grow.

Rees and I saturated newsagents with large, printed posters (those were the days, my friend), 'The Church and the Cotton Trade'. I do not know if either the Government or Methodism did anything to alleviate the situation. I greatly doubt it. But it made a good story, and we played it for all we were worth for some weeks.

A mild local furore was caused by an early interview with the Rev. Bertrand Coggle, an ardent Socialist, pacifist and total abstinence advocate, when I called upon him at his Walkden manse.

> Lancashire Methodism is fiddling while Rome burns,

he said – which made a good, arresting opening. He was referring to Saturday night concerts, plays, hot potato suppers and similar functions, which then (as perhaps now) played a large part in Northern church life. He continued:

> We have people who will pay ninepence for a concert and readily stay until past ten o'clock, and yet give one penny at the Sunday evening service and do not stay for the prayer meeting. It is lamentable that, while the issues of peace and

war are hanging by a thread, our Methodist Churches in this area would be absorbing their strength in dramatic societies and similar events.

He then went on to illustrate his thesis from accounts of such Methodist social events in the local paper. Unfortunately, all his examples were taken from the town's other Methodist circuit, which did not endear him to his colleagues there. Or perhaps fortunately, from the paper's viewpoint. A subsequent report headed 'Social Events and Spiritual Growth: Comments on a Recent Protest', stated:

> The Mosley Common Church, in the Walkden circuit, at which Mr Coggle is minister, has altogether dispensed with Saturday night concerts, hot potato suppers and similar functions which normally play so large a part in Lancashire Methodism. This was done because the officials considered that these events constituted a waste of church resources. As a result, it has been possible to concentrate much more on the spiritual and social work of the church than previously. The members of this church are mostly miners and weavers, and their strong interest in political affairs is traditional. Last January a three-week tour of Lancashire churches by Rev. Josef Stifter, a Czechoslovak minister, was the result of the initiative of the Mosley Common Peace Group.

Traditional Lancasire Methodism continued to flourish as the nearness of world conflict became monthly more apparent. Meanwhile, my column 'Lancashire Jottings' continued to record with careful detail the ephemera of chapel activities.

> Rev. Harold Thompson is indefatigable in his efforts to remedy the plight of the Blackburn folk (among whom he works and from whom he came) caused by the cotton depression. He tells me that a reply had been received to the second communication sent to the Premier asking if he would send a hopeful message to the ministers and clergy of the area.

I see that Rev. G. F. Stanley Atkinson, of the Southport (North) circuit, the Chairman of the Liverpool District, last week declared that Southport, with its encroachment on the Sabbath, was becoming less a place to which he would be attracted. At present, he added, it seemed determined to be a sixth-rate Blackpool. Mr Atkinson has just retired from the Presidency of the Southport and District Free Church Council, which the other day passed a resolution protesting against the recommendation of the Publicity and Attractions Committee that the Corporation's marine lake should be opened for boating on Sundays.

A minister's brother, Mr James Caro, was in that ominous year of 1939 pioneering a cinema Sunday School at Oldham. Rev. H. John Ivens in Southport was launching the 'Idealist Crusade', or 'Christian Patriotic Movement', which, he assured me,

leaves Conservatism and Liberalism far behind, but combines within itself the best elements of each. Catholics and Protestants, modernists and fundamentalists, join the movement without any surrender of belief. This, quite apart from the value of the actual crusading, is surely a great step forward on the road to Christian reunion.

The shilling badge was in the shape of a small shield in white enamel, with a cross behind a Union Jack, symbolizing

the spirit of the whole crusade, which seeks to inaugurate a new Christian patriotism.

He claimed that the crusade was broad in its

ecumenical nature, narrow in that it was a little bit Puritan. We rather revel in it. The pendulum has swung so very far, and maybe we shall have to be deliberately a little over-strict if we are to counteract the modern tendency. I want it to be a bit strict, a bit severe. On the other hand, it is in no way a repressive, but rather a liberating Puritanism.

As the year moved on to its inexorable tragedy, Harold Thompson continued to give me occasional 'copy' with his agitation about the cotton depression. The Bolton and Rochdale and North Lancashire Methodist Districts continued to attract large numbers to their Young Laymen's Missionary Conference and house party at Blackpool's Cliffe Hotel. Donald Soper spoke of 'the declension in the world of liberty and freedom' at a junior missionary rally at Manchester – an occasion, I wrote,

> always largely attended. Despite a recent severe illness, he was as vigorous and convincing as ever.

Sunday 3 September was still some months away. I carried on recording the ephemera of Northern Methodism in 'Lancashire Jottings'.

> I learn that ...
> I hear that ...
> The other day I was talking to ...

Motoring from my Bolton digs to Manchester on Wednesday 26 April I was startled to read on a newspaper poster 'Budget Shock for Motorists' and 'Conscription'.

The following Sunday, I went to a service at the Champness Hall, Rochdale, and saw Rev. J. Edward Eagles in vigorous pulpit action.

> Did Jesus Christ die to establish a fun fair?

he shouted, and went on:

> Please do not talk about dancing as having anything to do with the keep fit movement. Of all so-called recreations, the one that does most harm to the body is that which takes place in heated rooms and goes on far into the night, thus robbing young people of their needed sleep, and which constitutes no physical exercise at all.

It was an extraordinary performance. At times, he disappeared completely from view below the rostrum. Then he would suddenly reappear, his right hand held aloft, almost crying with emotion. He was not, I later discovered, when I met him at Cliff College, Derbyshire (the subject of a later chapter) remotely like this in private conversation but a quietly spoken, intelligent, friendly man. It has been a source of wonder to me why many preachers seem completely to change their personalities and voices (even when allowance has been made for the need to project) when preaching.

I longed to escape, as I was to do on so many occasions, from the stifling, claustrophobic atmosphere of the large Methodist Central Hall. The gregarious warmth of the congregation as they sang the great Wesley hymns, the near jollity of it all oppressed me deeply.

It was with relief that I came out into the Rochdale streets among, yet strangely apart from, the unchurched Lancashire lads and lasses. I longed to be part of them, to hail them as kindred spirits. They were free from the Methodist get-together, and I wanted to be one of their innocent, non-religious, non-worshipping fraternity. What appealed was their free spirits and above all their non-attachment.

And what repelled me about the righteous was not their dullness. For truly, they were not dull. Nor was it the self-righteousness of the unco-guid, a type I rarely encountered, happily a fast-dying species. It was the happiness akin to jollity that oppressed me. If I did not yearn to dwell in the tents of wickedness, even less did I want to be a doorkeeper in the house of the Lord. I wanted fresh air, and either no company at all or that of a few uncomplicated kindred spirits. But never, oh never, this H-A-P-P-Y thing. 'A lifetime of happiness!' protested a Shavian character, 'No man alive could bear it. It would be hell on earth.'

I was wearying of all those ardent renderings of 'O for a thousand tongues to sing' and 'O Thou who camest from above' beloved of rally organizers and attenders. I vowed that never would I choose them to be sung at any of my preaching appointments. Nor have I, after well over fifty years of being what Methodism calls a fully accredited local preacher. Nor would I have ever contemplated spending my holidays with a band of happy Wesley Guilders. Perhaps it is as well. I was to do all these things, go to all these places, professionally. But a reporter should be objective, standing apart and even if outwardly friendly and approachable, even if seeking to convey in his writing the atmosphere of the thing, yet inwardly aloof, feeling somewhat smugly superior. And this, I think, preserved my sanity.

Meanwhile, the churches prayed for peace and for the most part expected war. Conscription in any form was opposed by thirty-eight Hartley Victoria College (Manchester) students. 'We contend firmly' their letter ended 'that the regimentation of men and the denial of personality that is involved in obedience to the war machine is destructive of all those values which, as Christians, we seek to conserve.'

The Military Training Act was the subject of several resolutions in Lancashire. A young people's conference of Manchester's City Road Circuit urged the Government 'to act now in an effort to secure a just settlement of world affairs, not by force of arms and preparation to resist attack, but by constructive peace-making'.

The Co-ordinating Committee of the Merseyside Groups of the Peace Pledge Union asked Rev. Norman Glanville, of the Liverpool Mission, to express to the Government their regret that 'its policy of the neglect of the ways of peace has now felt compelled to adopt the conscription of manpower' and 'assure all men within the Merseyside area of their wholehearted support should any of them, by reason of conscience or from religious motives, feel called upon not to respond to the country's demand'.

Dr Maldwyn Edwards was appointed chairman of min isterial groups of the Methodist Peace Fellowship in the two Manchester Districts and 'proposed to have a service of information and help for conscientious objectors for a period of an hour or so each evening for the next month'.

In the issue of 22 June 1939 five girls, with their teacher, were pictured carrying, in a large letter each, the word P-E-A-C-E. The caption ran:

For over half a century the Free Churches of Openshaw, Manchester have organized a united Procession of Witness in the early Summer. This year, out of twelve churches taking part, five were Methodist. The picture shows some of the Methodist scholars in the procession displaying a plea for peace.

Alas, a disregarded plea!

In Liverpool, I called on Rev. W. Rutherford Basham, who later became an Anglican priest. He was shown in a picture in a later issue illustrating my interview, with his large unemployed men's fellowship at High Park Street. Many of the members were Communists or ex-Communists, free thinkers, sceptics, former fighters in the Spanish Civil War (which they became against Mr Basham's advice) and there was a forty-year-old unemployed man who supported a family of three.

I had gone to Liverpool from the Southport Convention, and stayed with the Bashams. On my first morning there, Rutherford Basham showed me round the new Anglican Cathedral, insisting that the early lady chapel illustrated the complexity of a young man's mind. The design, he said, grew simpler as the subject grew older. I did not know, nor do I now, what truth there was in that contention, nor recall how it impressed me at the time; I was twenty-four. I only know that in the afternoon I went to a cinema with Mrs Basham, and saw a film called *The Gaunt Stranger*. In the evening, I went to an open-air meeting and then a Communist came to supper. (He later became a Roman Catholic.)

One Sunday morning in Birmingham, I went to a civic service at St Martin's Church and heard a sermon by W. E. Barnes, in those days considered by many a dangerously unorthodox bishop, but whose views would hardly be considered heretical in this post *Honest To God* age. In the afternoon I went to a meeting of the Peace Pledge Union addressed by Wilfred Wellock. After tea at the Casino, I went first to a harvest festival service at the Methodist Central Hall, and from there went to the Paramount Cinema to see Oliver Hardy (with Harry Langdon instead of Stan Laurel) in *Elephants Never Forget* and a film called *Invitation to Happiness*.

At Liverpool Central Hall, I went to the first of the twenty Methodist Conferences I was to attend, the last being at Sheffield in 1980. I was also to report twenty-five Aggregates of the Local Preachers' Mutual Aid Association, thirteen Free Church Federal Council Congresses, ten Whitsun or Spring Bank Holiday weekends at Cliff College in Derbyshire, and nine Wesley Deaconess Convocations. They have said. What say they? Let them say.

That first Methodist Conference terrified me. In those days, proceedings were reported very fully, virtually in the style of *Hansard*. The conference was attended by 300 lay and 300 ministerial representatives. At that time the joint session preceded the purely ministerial one but this procedure was later wisely reversed. A team of *Recorder* reporters covered the proceedings by a system through which each did a 'take' of not more than twenty minutes and wrote it up, still at the press table just below the platform, with all the speeches and extraneous noises going on all round.

At Liverpool in 1939, the fullness of the reporting, even to the careful recording of 'laughter', 'loud laughter' and 'renewed laughter' and the complicated business, literally scared the wits out of me. 'Get that, Cock,' said Fred Everson, the ministerial team leader (whose regular contributions to the *Recorder* were often brilliant) seeing me pause in my none-too-efficient note taking.

This book is not a history of modern Methodism, the ecumenical movement, nor yet of the *Methodist Recorder*, but a purely personal reflection. In passing, I merely recall that the President of the Conference then was Rev. Richard Pyke. He commended the report on sex, which was an innocuous document by today's standards, although its approval of contraception shocked some representatives at the time.

When the outbreak of war became daily more certain, the Lancashire office had to be closed. I was kept on the *Recorder* staff *pro tem* at the same salary, and given a roving commission touring the Lancashire coast.

I drove into Southport one Saturday in August 1939. I looked in en route at Hesketh Bank, a lovely little village midway between Preston and Southport, paying a return visit to the sub-postmaster, Mr. T. M. Wright, who was the Methodist Chapel's society steward. I found him in the cricket field. In those days the village had three cricket teams which played in the Southport and District League. Three features characterized communal life there – temperance work, music and art.

Southport was packed with visitors. Police were directing motorists and pedestrians in Lord Street. Progress was almost impossible along the Promenade, especially near the Floral Gardens. After the Sunday evening service, there was a procession of witness from Christ Church for an interdenominational 'sands mission'. I left Southport noting the Convention of Religions held there, representing Christianity, Judaism, Mohammedanism, Hinduism, Confucianism, Buddhism and Taoism, organized chiefly by the English branch of the Vedanta Movement.

By the following Wednesday I was in Morecambe. The last weekend at Blackpool was doubly disquieting. Because of a growing awareness of the seriousness of political events there was the same oppressive atmosphere as precedes a storm. It was, I sensed, a desire to escape from reality rather than stoical calmness that attracted the thousands to Blackpool in August 1939, and this, it seemed to me, was the real reason for the slow emergence of crisis-consciousness.

I found, too, extravagance and vulgarity. It seemed as characteristic of Blackpool that it had spared no expense in acquiring Epstein's statue of Adam, as it was that a man stood outside shouting, 'Come 'n see Adam, girls'.

'It is impossible to forget that we meet in a time of extreme crisis,' said the minister at the evening service at the Central Methodist Church, adding, 'though this is a greatly overdone term.' The service ended with 'These things shall be: a loftier race', a hymn hardly ever sung now, and which had found its way into the 1933 hymn book in the teeth of great opposition from some members of the Hymn Book Committee of those days. Its sentiment is utopian rather than Christian. But the two are not mutually exclusive, and its rendering then was expressive of a faith that triumphed over even the inevitability of war. There were prayers for peace, and the minister quietly told the congregation what were the latest diplomatic moves. He said it was a false sense of values that tried to derive comfort from the Wayside Pulpit, 'Don't worry, it may never happen.' Then we went down to the beach for a short open-air service. It was a short one because the tide was coming in. Central Church, strategically placed, had been open for intercession for world peace ever since the crisis a year earlier. The open-air meeting was largely attended, and the increased sense of need caused by the tense situation meant that the speakers had a quiet, eager hearing. When at last the tide made it impossible to continue, heads were bared and bowed as, amidst the noise and lights of Blackpool, there were pronounced familiar words that had suddenly acquired new significance: 'May the peace of God be with you.'

Later, I was sent to a certain command's headquarters to find out what provisions were being made among the militiamen in camp. And I was continuing the rounds of mission anniversaries. 'New Occasions and New Duties at Bolton', 'Evangelism at Blackburn', 'Social and Evangelistic Service at Huddersfield', 'Practical Christianity at Leeds', 'Social and Spiritual Work in a Distressed Area' (Wigan). I went to the opening of a new church in Richmond, Yorkshire, where the total cost, including the value of the site, was £6,800 and of another at Ravenscliffe, Bradford, costing (with Sunday School buildings) £7,730.

My most interesting assignment in those days was an interview with writer Crichton Porteous. When I met him, he divided his time between writing and farming in Combe, an isolated village near Buxton. Here, too, he taught each Sunday in the little stone Methodist chapel, sometimes preaching to an evening congregation of eight.

It was not in his capacity as a Sunday School worker that I was anxious to see him. It was the countryman I wanted to meet – the countryman who had written two remarkable books, *Farmer's Creed* and *Teamsman*. I had heard much of him in Manchester. While a relatively young man he had shown his calibre by renouncing the certainty of inheriting a prosperous business and settling down to learn all that there was to know about crops and cattle and horses. He preferred getting up at six, in sunshine or in snow, and bringing in the cows to working in the Manchester office of his uncle.

He worked as a labourer on farms in Cheshire and in the Peak District, persevering at night with studies that would equip him as an agricultural correspondent. Then he became a reporter on Manchester papers, but after fourteen years gave that up to concentrate on writing.

I drove from Manchester after reading his vivid autobiography with clearly defined impressions in my mind of the farm high up in the gritstone country. I was eager to meet the farmer who read Ruskin, Chekov and Swift. I was eager to see for myself the cottage in which he lived, and the teamsmen, labourers, rabbit catchers, Irish casuals and the Mr Bone of *Farmer's Creed* who, with Goethe on his tongue, started life by selling manure at sixpence a barrow.

I was greeted at the door by a young man wearing breeches, a sports coat, an open-necked shirt and a disarming smile. He invited me into his study, and gave himself up to some hours of exhilarating talk about books, farming and Methodism.

About that period, I also interviewed Rev. James Laupmanis, a young, intense Russian Methodist minister. He was studying for his BA in Cardiff as well as travelling and lecturing. The *Recorder* had been right (on 23 May 1940) in calling his an 'amazing story'.

He had been imprisoned and suffered a knife wound in his shoulder and a cut over his eye while preaching at a Methodist mission at Maskauspriekspilseta. When he was six, his father was sent to Siberia, where he was killed. James was only seven when he began to earn his living. He worked on the land for long hours under a cruel and exacting master. He would sometimes rise at three o'clock and go out to the pastures, where he would later lead the cattle. Many evenings he would stay there, and as he watched the sunset he would quietly sing the Orphans' Song – which he translated into English for me and which I rendered in verse:

O setting sun, if you should see
My folk, bid them good-night for me.
As on your tireless course you run.
When in this place I shall awake
I'll think it is their kiss I take
Feeling your sunbeams kiss my face.

The story of his conversion was a dramatic one. But the interest then lay in his estimate of the growth of Methodism in every part of his country into a membership of several million. He also estimated that the Communist Party numbered only 4,000,000 out of a population of 185,000,000.

Those were for me days of almost unmitigated bliss. One day in particular stands out in my memory. The event was one of the least newsworthy I ever attended and the fact that I remember it so vividly cannot be explained simply by the fact that I have the short report and accompanying photograph in my cutting book. The same is true of hundreds of other happenings of far greater intrinsic interest.

The simple event was recorded in 'Lancashire Jottings', the northern edition feature which never really satisfied either Mr Wiseman or myself. It read:

> There is much to be said on both sides regarding the value and dangers of social activity in church life. No one can doubt that Rev. B. J. Coggle has indicated a real weakness of much northern church life. On Saturday I called in at the Wellington Street Church, Gorton, where the international bazaar was in process. I intended staying only a short while, but was so intrigued by the performance of Miss Pike's troupe that I stayed for the whole of the evening. There was the usual long interval, with what Lancashire folk modestly call refreshments handed round. I chatted with, amongst others, Mr Ralph Wagstaff, the youthful Sunday School secretary (who was gaily attired as a mandarin), and he told me of their flourishing school, and the Junior Christian Endeavour

which, though it had no stall at the bazaar, raised a considerable sum by a series of efforts.

The picture which accompanied my report showed a portly parson flanked by four ladies, three of whom were wearing indeterminate national costumes. The fourth, who had, I think, opened the bazaar was clutching a bouquet. It was captioned 'A snapshot at the Wellington Street International Bazaar, Gorton'.

In one of his hymns, Charles Wesley, with his love of paradox (in this case, more correctly oxymoron) has the startling phrase 'one eternal day'. This was that day for me although I was not then conscious of the fact. Perhaps it was of its very nature that I should not be aware of its significance, but my diary does something to confirm it:

> Morning in office. Afternoon, Renshaw (photographer) takes me first to Shaw for junior church altar, and then to Gorton international bazaar. I stay at latter, and see good child troupe. Enjoy myself.

Perhaps the whole of that period – so short in retrospect – held within itself a kind of 'eternal day'. I had never been so happy in my life. After a sterile period of unemployment, I was pioneering an experiment in religious journalism. I was doing it, without much instruction from head office, in my own way, on the whole to my own satisfaction and (more importantly) to the satisfaction of my beloved Chief, F. D. Wiseman. I was twenty-three, and I thought that it would last for ever.

But the date of that international bazaar was 29 April 1939. The following Thursday I was at the foot of the steps of Bolton Town Hall, listening to speakers calling for 'no conscription'. On the last day of August, at Mr Wiseman's behest, I went to western command headquarters at Chester in the morning and in the afternoon to a militia camp at Birkenhead.

The next day, Germany started bombing Poland, and I wrote my article on 'Methodism and Militia'. Two days later, a Sunday, Britain declared war on Germany.

I continued reporting mission anniversaries, church openings, and ecclesiastical conferences as if the future would be as idyllic as the immediate past. In my heart, I knew that my highest hopes, along with those of a million others, had already been dashed. But a few happy hours remain in some timeless dimension, forever spent by a carefree young man at the international bazaar at Wellington Street Methodist Church, Gorton.

3 Conscience in Wartime

On 9 March 1940, in accordance with a firm and long-standing conviction, I registered as a conscientious objector.

I had been one of the first signatories of the pledge that led to the formation of the Peace Pledge Union. A sermon preached by Dr H. Fosdick had inspired Canon Dick Sheppard to write a letter to national papers. The sermon had ended: 'I renounce war, and never again, directly or indirectly, will I sanction or support another. O, Unknown Soldier, in penitent reparation I make you that pledge.' The penultimate sentence was the wording of the pledge asking for postcard signatories to it. Although the letter was not prominently placed in the papers, Dick Sheppard soon received 30,000 replies.

For some time I agonized (in the company of John Rounsefell, then lately retired from the headmastership of Shebbear College, who was training me for my abortive candidature for the Methodist ministry) about the implications of 'directly or indirectly'. In the end we decided that the right course was to sign the peace pledge and cross that particular bridge when we came to it. In the event the PPU wisely dropped the clause.

I was summoned to the south west tribunal for conscientious objectors in Bristol. It was presided over by Judge Wethered, a former Quaker who had defected to the Church of England, who had a reputation for leniency toward conscientious objectors.

On the whole, pacifists had an easier time of it than their predecessors had had in the 1914–18 war. Four categories of conscientious objectors were recognized and I had opted for the most extreme, which was known as the 'absolutist' position. This meant that I would not be prepared to accept any direction for some form of alternative occupation in war time and the tribunal's satisfaction as to my sincerity upon this point was supposed to ensure my unconditional registration as a 'conshy'. My statement, formulated on the grounds of my Christian faith, was read out; then the judge cross-examined me. He was kind enough to say that there were no doubts in the minds of any on the tribunal as to my sincerity; but when I volunteered the statement that I realized I should have to undertake some form of employment before long, he seized on it and brushed aside my insistence on an absolutist claim.

They could not make up their minds about me, and asked me to return later. When I did, on 4 June 1940, I was told that I would be retained on the register of conscientious objectors conditional on my taking up some form of agricultural work. I soon decided not to exercise my right of appeal, thinking that to refuse to undertake such an activity, acceptable to me in itself, just because I had been ordered to do so, would be splitting hairs.

Five weeks and one day later, I began my work on a market garden in Penryn, near Falmouth, which was to last me for the duration of the war. My first morning in Cornwall was divided between hoeing and driving a tractor. There was the first of many air-raid warnings. Although there was to be relatively little actual damage or civilian casualties (in relation to the area's size and the number of alerts sounded), people were already leaving in droves, sometimes with bedding and other belongings piled high on top of their cars. On my first full day's work, my twenty-fifth birthday, I planted carrots, pulled cauliflower leaves, hoed, and carried potatoes. There was an air-raid on Falmouth, and I saw three boats hit in the harbour.

I scarcely knew a leek from an onion. Even when I was released six years later, although I had learnt much about the skills of the land (enough at least to grow vegetables in the garden of our Devon country cottage where we lived for a time) I had learnt much more about human nature. Meeting my future wife in Falmouth was, for me, the one unreservedly good thing that came out of those years.

On that first day, I diffidently met my fellow workmen. For the first time I was wearing working clothes – wellingtons, old grey flannels, an open-necked shirt. Later I wore breeches, leggings and hob-nail boots. It was July, and the sun was blazing down upon the fields of young plants. The horseman was ploughing, followed by the inevitable black crows and white gulls. Women and girls were weeding strawberries. Men were tending tomatoes in a row of thirteen greenhouses. A tractor could be heard in a higher field.

At my employer's suggestion, I had wandered around with a glorious inconsequentiality. Everyone was friendly and curious to meet the young greenhorn. Ned allowed me to take a hand at the plough. I was permitted to drive the tractor. I forked up some carrots. I helped the women hoe and weed the strawberries. I worked for the first of many, many times a strange contraption on two wheels called a 'planet hoe'. It seemed like a holiday, with the sun pouring down and the faintest suggestion of a breeze.

It became less like a holiday as month succeeded month and year succeeded year. I came to know every corner of every field by heart. I learnt the processes of the land, but never mastered them. I never learnt how to swing a hundredweight sack of potatoes over my shoulder and carry them in just the right way.

On the whole, I got on well with the regulars (there were also hordes of seasonal casuals) who worked alongside me all those long, long six years. A genuine camaraderie developed between us, and I was soon accepted. Sometimes when disagreements arose and tempers flew, my pacifism was raised as a taunt, and I was accused of being 'under the bloody umbrella' – but they were fully conscious of their own vulnerability in being engaged in a 'safe' reserved occupation.

Rosie, the female stand-by, had worked there, as had her mother before her, for longer than even the Boss could accurately recall. Her heart was as tender as her voice was raucous. Her almost incessant chatter could be heard several fields away. If she was alone, she would talk or sing to herself. Her musical repertoire ranged from 'Trust in the Lord and don't despair, He is a friend so true' to 'Roll me over in the clover, Roll me over, lay me down, and do it again'.

Teddy, who came from a neighbouring village, was the firm's lorry driver. In his mid-twenties, he was a fair-haired youth with a mischievous twinkle in his eyes and a missing front tooth. There were hints of his having once gone to Sunday School, but a less overtly religious person it would be impossible to imagine. I preferred him to most of the others.

His nickname was 'the Reverend', on the same principle by which one calls an elephant 'Tiny'. One Christmas, my future wife and I posted him a ministerial collar and stock which we had made. He wore it proudly at work all that day, as he cycled home and, as he afterwards related, at the village pub in the evening. 'When I went in first along, the landlord said, "What's the matter, Ted? Hurt yer neck?" So I took off me coat and said, "I'm a bloody parson now, so be careful of y'r bloody language."'

Alf Summers was the firm's veteran, a man in his sixties, whose hair was beginning to go grey. He had a weather beaten, bronzed complexion, sharp, angular features, hard glinting eyes, no teeth, and a perpetual dew-drop at the end of his nose. He was a Cornishman, but had years before worked in south Devon, and his slow, caustic speech was more Devonshire than Cornish. He had the well-earned reputation of being the firm's inveterate grumbler. He grumbled about the weather, the government, local administration, his wife's lodgers, his workmates, his employer. Most of the men disliked having to work alongside him. I rather enjoyed doing so – especially if we were left solely to each other's company.

One season, he and I dug potatoes together, day after day, week after week, month after month. ('Same job,' the boss would say, as we walked up the drive at seven-thirty each morning.) At those times, Alf kept up an endless flow of conversation which helped to make the long days speed past. And in all fairness, Alf was not always grumbling. Often he told stories of his own prowess in previous situations. He would tell the same story over and over again, and each time there was some detail added to it. He had a vivid imagination and an innate gift for narrative. He also appeared to have a prodigious memory. He would begin relating some minor incident of forty-five years before or so by saying, 'I remember one day in Paignton, oh about 1898 'twude be, and 'twas on a Saturday afternoon about ten past three, and I was in the bar parlour of the Gerston Hotel in Paignton . . .' He said he would drive passengers from the station to the hotel in the horse cabs of the period. As he talked, I could see the young Alf Summers, before the first world war, with his top hat, riding coat and whip. Years ago, he had worked at the Gerston Hotel: and he told me over and over again of the gargantuan tips he received then. When, after the war, I went to Paignton, my first wish was to find the Gerston Hotel. It was almost literally a stone's throw from the station.

As Alf related his endless store of anecdotes, it was an almost Dickensian scene that he conjured up. My favourite story was of the occasion when young Alf Summers and another young 'blood' had 'got off with' two young women in a south Devon pub. Both were attractive, flirtatious, and well-to-do. One indeed was a wealthy young widow. They invited Alf and his friend to their country house. (Here would follow detailed descriptions of the magnificence of this establishment.) Alf had been left with the wealthy young widow in the drawing room, drinking sherry. His pal had gone with the younger one through the French windows, and they had settled themselves upon a garden seat. Here, encouraged by the young woman's friendliness, the youth had gone too far in his advances and was making invasions of her clothing when, said Alf, 'She picked up a conger eel that was handy by and smacked him across the face with it.' 'Christ!' he would chuckle with appreciative reminiscence, 'all wet and floppy!' I never tired of hearing that one, and never ceased to marvel at the providence that so thoughtfully placed that conger eel 'handy by' to assist enraged womanhood to defend her threatened virginity.

In the haze of nostalgia, I think of those six years in the deceptive terms of 'these I have loved'. And indeed, it hadn't all been bad. When it ended, I knew there was much I would always look back upon with a measure of affection: Rosie bringing round the steaming cocoa at ten o'clock; the warmth of the sun on the back of my neck; working with the horseman in one of his good-tempered moods, which usually meant spending some of the day leaning against the cart and yarning; Alf Summers scraping the rotten parts off the parsnips with his knife, and chortling, 'Hair cut and shave – next please!' And I shall never forget the joy of unlacing hobnailed boots at the weekend.

But now I had taken them off for ever, and I was glad beyond measure, for there was so much I would be happy to leave behind: wheeling earth out of and into greenhouses on hot summer days; trimming hedges; forking up parsnips in rain-soaked soil; weeding on bitterly cold days. I would not miss cutting or carrying broccoli in the pouring rain, clad in oilers and heavy manure bags. I would not miss the freezing wind, the pouring rain, the blazing heat, the mud, the frost and the aching limbs. I would not miss working with the horseman in one of his bad tempered moods or the boss shouting, 'Oi! Oi! Douglas – leave that job now and carry on with the potato lifting.' It was all over and I was leaving it all behind – the sweat and the cold, the dust and the mud, the stinging nettles and the docks, the crops and the weeds.

In 1942 I had had a letter from F. D. Wiseman, assuring me of a welcome back to the *Recorder* after the war, if I so wished. At that time it already seemed as if I had been market gardening for decades, and the armistice seemed an eternity away. He for his part said:

I would far rather be whistling at the horses in the plough or grooming them, or tending tomatoes in a greenhouse, than sitting day by day in an office in work of doubtful national value and of very doubtful Christian value. If I were digging vegetables I should have time to think and make up my mind; at present I haven't; with the result that I can only see a brick wall in front of me and haven't time to devise a strategy for getting around it.

The brick wall is the institutionalism of the church and the degeneration of the British people (including myself). The two things are bricks and mortar, closely connected. If the nation woke up, or if the church woke up, there would be great hope. I had an idea that Singapore might arouse the nation and wrote in that strain in the 'Notes'. I thought that perhaps the defection of Burma, and even of India, might stir us to a consciousness of our easy-going existence and shortcomings; but there is little sign of it. And all the while the church – Methodist and other – just jogs along, singing its irrelevant hymns, preaching its unprophetic sermons, while the devil laughs and sniggers at its self-dupery. I don't feel that I am pulling my weight either personally or in the paper. I cannot personally, because I have no opportunity, and when I make an opportunity as at the Quarterly Meeting last December the superintendent says, 'A great speech,' someone else (a pacifist) says, 'Right on the nail,' and then we go on to the next business, which is the appointment of some committee. I cannot do so in the paper, because the editorial committee doesn't like it; it does not agree that Methodism just does not know where it wants to go or what it wants to do. All that matters is that Methodism should keep going, power-driven by its own money-machine, and hitched to the star of God so far as formal worship, emotional observances and holy prating can hitch it. So one just tries to lose oneself in a little more ARP work, in getting up a local Cadet Corps, in starting a Youth Centre, and what not – anything to keep the mind off the lowering sky, like one makes a loud cough when crunching a beetle underfoot. Oh no – it isn't defeatism. We may win the war; in fact, if Russia holds on, I think we shall. But unless something else happens in the meantime, the last state will be worse than the first.

I think, re-reading your letter, that you may wonder sometimes whether there is a place for you on the Recorder *after the war. There will be, and a warm welcome. I am looking forward to a much more progressive news policy when the chance comes. The Lancashire office was an experiment. It did not have time to mature, but it showed every sign of doing well. At any rate – if I am here after the war – I intend that the experiment shall not merely be renewed, but developed, with offices at Leeds and Plymouth (or Bristol) as well; and you, if you are wishful, shall be in with us. If we can't wake the church up editorially, we can through news. Hail the day!*

I like to think that, in some measure, we did rouse the church, and that in this I played some small part.

4 Recording Methodism

Immediately after the war, having had a brief spell in Fleet Street, I opened the *Methodist Recorder* northern counties' office on the premises of Oxford Place Chapel, Leeds.

Some time previously, there had been a number of Christian Commando campaigns, when teams of parsons and laymen invaded the secular world in its natural habitat rather than inviting the unchurched to traditional ten-day missions in churches, conducted by visiting charismatic evangelists.

It seemed to me that it would be pertinent to examine their effects upon the localities in which they had operated some considerable time afterwards, as well as reporting simultaneously on follow-up campaigns. There had, for instance, been such a campaign in Leeds at the beginning of 1945 where, in spite of a blizzard, about 1,200 people had gone to the opening meeting at Oxford Place Chapel. It had been hoped that the Anglicans would join forces. But the requirements of the new Education Act so absorbed their attention that they decided to take no active part.

The teams visited 97 factories, 12 secondary schools and the university. Services were held in cinemas every afternoon and evening, and there were visits to workers' canteens. At the final meeting in Brunswick Church, attended by about 1,300 people, 47 decisions were registered, making a total of over 400 decisions for the whole campaign.

Regular meetings for new converts were held for some months afterwards. Rev. Christopher Bacon carried on a class attended by 70 to 80 men at the municipal electricity power works. Something similar happened at a modern, high-class garment factory. Some ministers continued regular visits to factories, canteens, shops and the like, and took the gospel into modern industry.

The scale of the follow-up in relation to the size of the attack seemed pitiful. I wrote:

> Moreover a tremendous opportunity appears to have been missed with regard to the schools. After the campaign, ministers had the chance of going into some of the secondary schools. No advantage was taken of this splendid opportunity, because (so I was told) 'the number of ministers suitable for this kind of work is few, and all of them are busy'.

One minister who shared in visits to Leeds cinemas said they had been 'in the nature of a stunt or music-hall turn'. Most of the criticism came from folk in the churches, particularly parsons.

> One hears it said that they take up a considerable amount of a minister's time which might be better employed in tending his own flock; that they are expensive, and that the money has to be obtained from people already giving generously in other ways; that it is not always the churches who put in the most work for these campaigns who reap the benefit – and so on. It is the 'outsider' who seems to be favourably impressed at the church's concern about the common people, and their only criticism is that this kind of thing has not been done before.

Visits to the southern part of the country – Bristol, Chew Magna and Weston-super-Mare – and also to Grimsby, produced on the whole reassuring reports that showed some attention to John Wesley's dictum, 'I resolve not to strike one blow where I cannot follow the blow.' But it was at York that I discovered how sensitive the clergy could be to even the mildest criticism.

I had gone to a reunion rally (a sequel to a recent campaign) in the Odeon Cinema. Fifteen minutes before the meeting was due to start, the stalls were nearly filled with folk who had come from evening worship as well as (hopefully) the unchurched. On to the stage from the wings trooped three robed, unsmiling parsons, looking for all the world like the trial scene from Shaw's *Saint Joan*. There was a hymn and a prayer, and the chairman introduced the two speakers, both (as I conceded) admirably suited to address such a meeting. But I was appalled by the unimaginative, formal presentation – and said so.

Later, I visited Rowntree's cocoa works, where campaigners had spoken to 5,000 workers. Some spoke appreciatively of the visit but most gave me the impression that when the 'commandos' had gone, they almost immediately ceased to be even a topic of conversation. Many were offended at the intrusion into the canteen during their lunch break and one man unanswerably asked me, 'How would you like it, mister, if a parson butted in on you when you were having your dinner and started preaching to you?'

The girls were unreservedly enthusiastic and less varied in their comments. To my query, 'What did you think of the commandos?' they would reply, 'Oh, they were ever so nice. It was ever so interesting. There was no beating about the bush with them, if you know what I mean. They spoke straight out. One man was ever so witty, too. He made you laugh, but he made you think about what he was driving at, if I make my meaning clear. The things they talked about were just like real life. I hope they'll come again.'

A letter appeared in the *Recorder* from several of the ministers, strongly criticizing my report of all this. When I told Mr Wiseman that I had been taken aback at its virulence, he said they had earlier submitted a much more strongly worded one. He told them he would print it if they insisted, but advised them (in their own interests) to substitute a modified version. He exonerated me from any blame for reporting my honest impressions and findings. Every *Recorder* editor has always stood by his staff, unless he had strong reason to believe one of them had let him down.

Methodist ministers (for whom I gained a tremendous respect over the years) tend on the whole to be ultra-sensitive to criticism and often jealous of others' success stories – often rationalizing their criticisms in high-sounding spiritual vocabularies.

Radical change came slowly to Methodism in theology, in evangelicalism, in method and in day-to-day church life. It seemed at first very much 'business as usual' and I observed and reported it in only slightly less fulsome terms than I had done in that brief pre-war spell in Manchester. But I was sincerely trying to be objective and to record what I found, warts and all.

Rev. F. H. Everson was touring the country with his 'How Great a Flame' exhibition of Methodist work and witness. Newark launched 'England's First United Christian Youth Week'. I attributed its success to the organizing ability of Mr Douglas Blatherwick, a future Vice-President of the Methodist Conference. Together with fellow 'Westminster Laymen' (one of whom, Eric Piggott, was then assistant editor of the *Recorder*) he was to present the church with a by no means ignored challenge. Church centenaries were ten a penny at that time. I remember that the centenary of Haworth church coincided with the bicentenary of the society and the seventy-fifth anniversary of the formation of the Haworth and Oakworth circuit. 'Centenary in Brontë Land' was the inevitable heading.

I found Rev. Bertrand Coggle still living in the manse where I had called upon him before the war. He was by then in his tenth and last year in the Walkden circuit. I was quite unreasonably amazed at this. It seemed to me that a whole lifetime had elapsed during my few years on that market garden.

> He greeted me, rather surprisingly, with, 'I thought you were the man from Littlewoods.' This he later explained by referring to a public meeting to be held at the Walkden Co-operative Hall under the auspices of the Walkden and Worsley Christian Union and Youth Council on Monday 18 November. He is then to preside over a meeting addressed by Canon Peter Green and Rev. E. Benson Perkins, both of Manchester, to attack the gambling menace. He showed me his bills with the slogan 'Gambling – a Vicious Circle'. This is a play on the Littlewoods Pools slogan 'Join the Happy Circle'.

It was my turn to be enigmatic. 'Is Lancashire Methodism still fiddling while Rome burns?' I asked. In 1939 Mr Coggle had declared that it was; and had gone on to protest against the emphasis Lancashire Methodism placed on its social activities, almost to the exclusion of its spiritual mission. 'There is not a single regular prayer meeting in my circuit,' he had then declared, and had continued, 'Some of our churches even spend the Lord's Day organizing financial efforts.'

He smiled now, and replied: 'Too much emphasis is still being put upon the wrong things to the neglect of Sunday worship.'

But he went on to give a more positive report of local church life, especially in relation to its youth activity.

Little had really changed since pre-war days. I had the feeling that the church had been marking time for the duration. Despite Hiroshima, there was virtually as little apprehension about the future as there had been in church life a few years before 1939. It was not only Lancashire Methodism that was fiddling and ignoring the very threat of nuclear disaster.

The ecumenical movement, by no means young, had not yet seriously penetrated grass-roots consciousness. The youth movement, in the form of the Methodist Association of Youth Clubs, was beginning to spread its wings. *Young Britain*, the *Recorder*'s youth page, regularly carried the feature 'The Ace of Clubs' (the retention of 'The' was typical of the prevailing influence of pre-war journalism), with its fulsome write-ups and massed formation photographs.

Rev. William Wallace, later to be killed in a train disaster, was holding public debates in Sheffield's Victoria Hall opposing the motion of a city councillor 'that Sunday games in parks be permitted' and speaking against the motion of the chairman of the Sheffield branch of the Secular Society 'that Christianity is the historic enemy of progress'. 'I think these public debates must be continued,' said Mr Wallace before the crowd dispersed, 'for we seem to have found a technique here that is going to be helpful to everyone concerned. I should like a debate on the question of Sunday cinemas with the Chairman of the Cinematograph Exhibitors' Association.'

This was very much a contemporary issue. Grimsby, I reported, became the first town in the country in which the churches and the cinemas reached agreement. During emergency powers, cinemas had been opened there on Sundays, an arrangement which stood until the end of 1947. Because they were opened as a war-time measure, the Home Office sent out to councils the statement that if Sunday cinemas were desired, they would have to make special application.

A town meeting was held in Grimsby Town Hall, attended by about 150 people. This turned out to be a rowdy affair, at which (by a show of hands) Sunday opening was decided upon by a narrow majority. Christian bodies agreed to withhold their right to demand a poll on the issue.

Rev. David Edwards of Grimsby Central Hall, showed a great readiness to be interviewed. When I said I would not quote him unless he so desired, he said with some emphasis, 'But I want to make a statement.' This refreshing frankness was in contrast to the usual practice of many Methodist ministers who would begin by demurring, insisting that they were not of that breed of their contemporaries who sought *Recorder* publicity and would then proceed to provide me with enough material to fill three-quarters of a page.

He told me that the Public Relations Officer and the cinema managers felt that if the churches insisted on demanding a poll there would be a bitter fight and a good deal of acrimony in the town. So ministers and clergy decided to co-operate. They placed before the Exhibitors' Association a series of proposals. They urged a later hour of opening and only one showing on Sunday, and that no children under sixteen should be admitted. They suggested that there should be a joint committee of cinema managers and clergy to raise the standard of films generally, particularly those shown on Sunday. These proposals were thrown out by the Exhibitors' Association as well as the proposal to allow clergy to address cinema audiences. The independent cinemas were willing to offer their facilities, but the 'combines' felt that to allow parsons to come in would open the door to all sorts of organizations who wanted to speak in the cinemas.

Faced with this, the churches decided to waive their democratic right to insist upon a poll. 'We felt,' said Mr Edwards, 'it would only widen the gulf between the pagans and the churches. We wanted to avoid a bitter fight over this matter, and we felt sure that they would win anyway.'

Realism won the day in Grimsby. 'Had we indeed managed to enforce the closing of Sunday cinemas,' said Mr Edwards, 'we should have eighteen thousand people outside. Where would they go? A majority would have been found in clubs, pubs, and walking the streets; and we should have been creating another problem for ourselves. So, on balance, we decided not to demand a poll, but to seek closer co-operation.'

It was beginning to dawn upon the Christian consciousness that the whole issue of Sunday observance had to be rethought.

> The railway and road transport are a menace to our Sundays in the summer with their summer trips. We seem to be unable to do anything about that. In this quarter of the town we have many people living three or four families in one house. Yet many of those living in our suburbs, including even Christian people, come out in their cars on Sundays, and are yet horrified at the thought of the opening of Sunday cinemas. Opposite the Regal Cinema (itself near the Central Hall) there are gambling saloons open on a Sunday. The Cleethorpes fun-fairs are crowded with young folk. We are doing nothing at all about that.

At Rotherham, cinema managers and representatives of the Anglican Chapter and the Ministers' Free Church Fraternal agreed 'that Sunday opening be limited to evening performances; that two representatives, one Anglican and one Free Church minister, should be available for consultation as to the type of film to be shown'.

In Bolton, the churches took a more militant line, and

strongly opposed Sunday cinema opening. In spite of pouring rain the Albert Hall was packed to hear eleven speakers give five-minute addresses. There was a vote by show of hands which, by a majority of about two to one, rejected the Council's decision to apply for Sunday opening. A petition for a poll was presented to the Mayor the next morning.

> Controversy continued to rage. Clergy and ministers expressed their views in the pulpit or the church magazine. Vicars became voluble in large numbers, but so did the non-churchgoing layman. One of the more constructive and challenging suggestions was that the churches, if they were going to oppose Sunday cinemas, should do more to attract young people in their own towns and villages.
>
> The holder of this view continued, 'Couldn't each church have a Sunday evening youth club, perhaps from eight o'clock until ten o'clock with knitting classes for the girls and handicrafts for the boys, or even debates on current affairs? Most young people, like myself and my friends, attend night classes at least three times a week, and are only able to get together on Saturdays and Sundays. If the churches took this step it would prevent thousands of young people from crowding into snack bars, cinemas, and pubs, and walking the streets ...'

My report continued:

> Counting of the votes began in the Albert Hall at 10 am on Tuesday 10 December. The result of the poll, announced by the Mayor, was 28,999 in favour of Sunday cinemas and 17,601 against, giving a majority in favour of 11,398. 'That is the whole of the business,' said the Mayor, and the protagonists quietly dispersed, without any demonstration.

In Huddersfield, where Sunday opening had existed for five years, churches rejected an offer of co-operation from the local Cinemas Association. Its secretary, also a cinema manager, said their committee's recommendations included 'that no application should be made for hours of opening that would interfere with the activities of the Sunday Schools'. They met the churches, who firmly refused the offer, leading the cinema manager to say, 'We did not want to fight the churches at all; indeed, we did not desire a poll on the matter, and would have preferred some form of compromise settlement. After all, cinemas have been opening on Sundays in Huddersfield for five years; it is a bit late in the day suddenly to discover that this practice is going to bring us all to perdition.'

A meeting to debate the matter was held in the Town Hall, which was almost full. At the close, a vote was taken. There were 427 in favour of Sunday opening, and 496 against. This was not, however, the town vote (which took place a few days later, and which appears to have been unreported in the *Recorder*).

In Exeter at the public meeting the vote was against the retention of Sunday cinemas, but at the subsequent poll the vote was overwhelmingly in favour.

This seems to have been the almost invariable outcome in days when television had not yet become a powerful counter-attraction and, in the words of an Exeter Methodist minister of those days, the voting at public meetings probably was influenced by the fact that 'church people were already in the habit of going to public meetings, and so had turned up in larger numbers than the non-churchgoers'.

In the north Devon resort of Ilfracombe, although the Methodist superintendent minister told me he had desired co-operation with the cinema proprietors to ensure a more efficient control of Sunday films, opposition was organized by members of the Free Church Council, one of whom paraded the streets with sandwich boards. Here Sunday opening won the day by a majority of 500 votes.

Rotherham's churches decided against opposition.

After consideration, it was agreed that Sunday opening should be limited to evening performances, that two representatives – one Anglican and one Free Church minister – should be available for consultation as to the type of film to be shown, and that on special days a church representative might be invited to hold a short service during the Sunday evening performance.

On the National Day of Prayer, ministers addressed audiences in three Rotherham cinemas.

After a brief address in the middle of one of the programmes Rev. Walter Budd invited the audience to join him in repeating the Lord's Prayer, which they did. 'We were very well received both by the audience and the cinema managers,' he said, 'and the managers have expressed their willingness for us to do the same sort of thing again.'

After that, the matter seems to have been dropped. 'The Growing Menace of Gambling' was the theme of a protest rally at Walkden when the large Co-operative Hall was packed to hear Canon Peter Green and Rev. E. Benson Perkins attack 'the recent tremendous growth of this national evil, especially through the medium of football pools'. Bingo as we now know it had scarcely yet penetrated. Meanwhile, for good or ill, Sunday cinemas were firmly established (though today, cinema after cinema has been converted into a bingo hall).

By 1949 I had been married for over a year, working from the *Recorder*'s west country office in Exeter. 'What Have the Commando Campaigns Left Behind Them?' asked a heading in the 5 May issue of that year of my report of what I had found in the west of England and south Wales.

This seems to have been rather more encouraging than earlier enquiries further north. Visits were still made regularly by a padré to the Lawrence Hill depot canteen of the Bristol Tramways and Carriage Company following the Christian Commando campaign in the city in 1944. This had created something of a stir at the time and some resentment among some workers. Now the padré was well received, taking part in services, debates, quizzes, brains trusts and discussions.

The commandos' entry into the Royal Dockyard was seen as the principal achievement of the Plymouth campaign of 1946.

> To have permission to enter a naval establishment of that kind was almost without precedent. Indeed, permission was at first refused. But once in, they visited every part of the Yard, as well as the canteens. They were not, however, allowed to follow it up with factory and canteen padréships. (There is an Anglican padré there already.) Indeed, an exhaustive inquiry has produced no evidence of any padréships of that kind in the whole of Plymouth. This seems to be due less to lack of enthusiasm on the part of local ministers than to a definite dislike of such intrusions on the part of the management of the big stores and other places.

A different strategy was devised of Christian community cells and

> when Dr Donald Soper later visited the city with the Order of Christian Witness he found the ground well prepared by keen young people meeting regularly for Bible study, fellowship and prayer and eager to co-operate.

Two years after the Rhondda Valley campaign, the most notable piece of follow-up work appeared to be

> at the Polikoff clothing factory in Treorchy, started by Rev. Edward Avery ... insofar as the spirit of the campaign has continued, it has made itself manifest mainly through the witness of the Tonypandy Central Hall, for years a recognized social as well as spiritual centre of the valley. Unfortunately co-operation between Christian denominations was almost entirely confined to the days of the campaign and immediately beforehand. When it was over, they returned to their former seclusion. There is a marked difference between the co-operative action of the Bristol churches and the segregation of the Rhondda Valley clergy.

> Wherever campaigns were held in southern England and Wales, they demonstrated that the churches were equipped to let the people see that they were prepared to go among them, and corrected many erroneous ideas about ministers and organized religion.

By and large, the Christian Commandos had no more and perhaps no less effect upon the spiritual climate of the land than did the more publicized visits of Dr Billy Graham. Lord Soper, writing thirty years after he was President of the Methodist Conference, summed it up with customary succinctness: 'Much-vaunted evangelical campaigns have come and gone and yet the general situation today is more or less the same as that which greeted Billy Graham whose first excursion was in 1954 when I was in the Chair.'

At that earlier time, Eric Pigott commissioned different writers to cover Billy Graham's Harringay and Earls Court rallies, including all the paper's staff reporters. From the outset it was made clear that each writer had a completely free hand and that the paper took no official line, either for or against Billy Graham.

It was in the 1960s at Earls Court that I reported the Graham phenomenon. My first visit I found (in words picked out for the two headings) to be 'respectable' and 'decorous'. I was not conscious of many, if any, non-churchgoing types, and the first half of the evening was remarkable for the quietness and restraint of the massive congregation. The singing of familiar hymns

> lacked the rousing quality one often finds in religious gatherings of a less avowedly evangelistic kind ... Dr Graham suddenly appeared as if from nowhere, and after silent prayer and a brief introductory word, went straight into action.
>
> His theme was life after death and his text was taken from (of all books for such a theme) Ecclesiastes 3.2: 'a time to die'. The address was given in his characteristic style, taking illustrations from a wide field that ranged from many personal experiences to the exegesis of John Stott.

He concentrated perhaps too much on the certainty of death for every man. 'If we could come back here in a hundred year's time, we should all be skeletons.' Looking across those serried ranks, the mental image this conjured up was something more grisly than was ever thought up by any producer of any X-certificate films.

Later came the inevitable appeal. 'Are you prepared to live and die? You can decide tonight.'

The appeal made, there was a second's pause, and then quietly, without another word being spoken or music being played or sung, they moved almost noiselessly forward, 1,082 of them, to stand silently before the platform. They came from the side seats, from the main body of the hall, from the adjoining auditorium where they had been taking part through closed-circuit television. They listened to a few simple but sound words of helpfulness, then filed away to meet their counsellors.

There was a short closing prayer from General Frederick Coutts, the international leader of the Salvation Army, and a member of the Crusade Council of Reference, and the rest of us walked out to enter the waiting coaches and cars, or to be transported underground into the London night.

That was on 4 June 1966. A June evening a year later found Billy Graham back to a good first night for his campaign which was fast becoming an annual event. The slogan 'Billy's back' he twice disowned that evening, though somewhat inconsistently he first attributed it to a British advertising agency and later said, 'I don't know who thought up that one.'

It was with a sense of being present at the first night of the season, albeit a much shorter one than last year's, that I settled into my reserved press seat. It was much more like the first night of the Proms (and certainly not the last night of the Proms) than the opening of a jazz festival.

There were again the pale blue curtains bearing in large, darker blue lettering the inscription 'Jesus said, "I am the way, the truth and the life" John 4.6'. Immediately in front was the 2,000 strong choir, the men in black, the ladies in white. In front of these was the dais with its reading desk, grand piano, electronic equipment for relaying; there were several familiar personalities and the inevitable bishop to pronounce the benediction.

The auditorium was probably three-quarters full and as its audience capacity is 19,000 it was an impressive sight, crying out for colour television.

When the great moment arrived, there was a reverent hush of expectancy. Not even his most impassioned utterances were punctuated by so much as an 'Amen' or a 'Hallelujah'. It would have been akin to cheering in the middle of a Beethoven concerto. Only one of the many young people present I saw reminded me of the last night of the Proms. He was two rows in front of me, and the back of his pale green jacket bore the CND emblem, and the words 'Lord Nice. It's people I can't stand. Down with war'. His attentiveness, however, was beyond reproach.

Just before the appeal proper Dr Graham said, 'There is an old man here of seventy-four who has rejected Christ for sixty years. It isn't easy to get through to a man who has rejected Christ for as long as that. Sir, if there is any wavering or stirring in your heart, you had better come.' At once, a little elderly gentleman rose from a front seat, and came forward.

Then came the expected formula: 'I'm going to ask you to get up out of your seats. Hundreds of you.' Without a pause, silently, there in Earls Court, 650 did just that (as did 1,100 altogether at the relays).

The demonstration was short-lived. As soon as the appeal was over, four young men walked toward the dais with placards reading 'US killers get out of Vietnam'. Billy didn't bat an eyelid, nor did anyone else give the least indication that they were aware of anything untoward – neither the thousands in their seats nor the hundreds moving almost noiselessly forward.

> Only the pressmen round me showed their first sign of animation. Stewards moved quickly forward, held the intruders in expert, vice-like grips and ejected them. It was over in seconds. People were still moving forward to the base of the dais as if nothing had happened.

It had been a good first night.

When I opened the paper's western counties office after the war, redundancy was still the unhappy legacy of the reunion of the divisions of Methodism in 1932. There were, and in some instances still are, small towns and villages with two or more (usually ex-Wesleyan and ex-United Methodist) chapels, both with sparse congregations, each steadfastly refusing to close.

I once went to a Cornish town, with crusading zeal and armed with jealous care, to expose the infamy of local redundancy. I called on two ministers, but failed to locate the laymen I wanted to see. No one had been forewarned of my visit.

By the first post the next morning, I received an anonymous letter which ended

'I would rather go to Hell on my own than to Heaven in the company of those who want to close our chapel.
Yours in his service,
A Lifelong Methodist'

A typical report of mine in those days read:

> Two nearby Methodist churches in one small town, each with an average Sunday congregation that would barely half fill the smaller of the two buildings, is an only too common situation throughout the country sixteen years after Methodist union.

I did the rounds of the lay folk.

> 'It would be a bad day's work if either place should close,' said one. 'For the sake of Methodism we feel we must keep

going, and I am dead against closing our place. I do not believe that union is either practicable or desirable, and I hope it will not come in my lifetime.'

But it did. The church he attended was sold to the Brethren, and he worshipped happily at the other until his death.

A more realistic attitude had been taken by another layman, who had said, 'It is foolish to have two buildings, both of which are expensive to run. Unfortunately there are people in both churches who would not be prepared to worship at the other. But union is bound to come here eventually.'

One Sunday evening in 1947, before leaving the northern counties office, I went to services in five different chapels in Brimington, near Chesterfield, just to prove that the thing could be done. It was a quiet, straggling village, and visitors to any of its five Methodist chapels must have been rare. At each, I was received with great courtesy and some surprise, and conducted carefully to a pew. With still greater surprise, I was observed only a few minutes later creeping quietly out. I landed myself for two collections, several hymns, and parts of two sermons. I should not be surprised to learn that, all these years later, a subject of occasional conversation there is still the odd behaviour of a strange young man one Sunday evening.

On the whole, the redundancy problem has been greatly reduced since those days. A few stubborn cases remain – and I have no idea how it fares these days at Brimington.

By 1974 I was witnessing Sheffield's Urban Theology Unit, under the directorship of Dr John Vincent. This I saw as Christian radicalism in action in a much neglected inner city environment at Pitsmoor. The choice of site was strategic rather than theological, though the Urban Theology Unit was 'convinced a warped understanding of the gospel had allowed it to be perpetuated only where financial, cultural and social acceptance still support it, and that the state accepts assumptions about the church's privileged presence because "it wants shepherds for the people, but tends to react violently against prophets"'. They were 'engaged in endless debates with councillors, planners, community developers and sociologists'.

At that time, UTU had 550 members in this country engaged in theological studies in practical contemporary settings, action groups with community organizations, urban ministry courses, post-graduate years primarily for theology undergraduates, and lay training courses. I met a very mixed group of people on the two days of my visit. (I stayed the night at John Vincent's manse.) They were of all denominations, of course, mostly leftish intellectuals.

> I sat in on a penetrating study of Romans 13 and John Howard Yoder's *The Politics of Jesus*, led by Rev. E. S. Howard Kessler, an Anglican diocesan planning officer in Durham, who has worked for ten years in America as a planning consultant, and on a session led by Dr Vincent on Ivan Illich's *Deschooling Society*.
>
> UTU's prophets believe in acting parables by 'involvement' – the word is threadbare but in this context unavoidable – in such environmental concerns as getting rid of smoke and filth, supporting the rephasing of housing, and opposing racial discrimination.
>
> It would be easy to write off these not-so-reluctant radicals as peremptorily as H. G. Wells did the early Fabians, contrasting their puny numbers with the magnitude of their task. It would be easy to debunk their zealous activity after the manner of Malcolm Muggeridge's self-deprecating autobiography *Chronicles of Wasted Time*. The 'Jesus Thing' radicals are not wasting their time or that of the church, and may well be seen in retrospect to have made an invaluable contribution.
>
> Meanwhile, their theological emphasis could well be balanced by a dose of, say, P. T. Forsyth, and their activism by the Christian passivism (in their terms a heresy) of Oswald Chambers, still the least intolerant and most perceptive of conservative evangelicals. ('Practical work may be a competitor against abandonment to God.')

An infectious air of immediacy pervades the Urban Theology Unit in the Pitsmoor area of Sheffield. Even during so flying a visit as mine, there was a certain sense of bliss at being alive in such a dawn, and those whose seniority debars them from finding it 'very heaven' have their own mellowed brand of crusading zeal. The surroundings and inner city environment are not without their sombre aspects, but nor, perhaps, was the French Revolution.

This is not meant to be condescending. There is ample evidence that the Sheffield Inner City Ecumenical Mission — the name of the circuit of which Dr John Vincent is superintendent — the Ashram Community Trust, and UTU, which more or less overlap, are engaged in highly significant Christian enterprises, as seen in part by the daunting mass of publications continuously churned out.

There is no lack of documentation; and it is all to the good that twentieth century incarnational Christianity should be presented as essentially revolutionary.

If the Pitsmoor revolutionaries have their way, a good many heads will roll. Their *Ministry in Cities* report calls for new directions and radical reorientation to deal with the present crisis. In the report, they explicitly repudiate the Church Unity movement and the concepts of a Church Building, Planning and Strategy Ministry as a fixed function or calling, and Christendom, with its typical assumptions that a Christian land needs places of worship.

Each of these negations is followed by an affirmative, such as, 'We believe that churches should close and sell their buildings, but move back into the streets, the neighbourhoods, and the communities they originally came from, using community rooms, clubs, public houses, schools, associations etc. wherever possible, and putting what personnel they have into experimental forms of "church" in community houses, shop fronts, service centres, church houses, etc.'

Experimental post-graduate courses have dealt with development and liberation, doing theology in the city (a review of ways of bringing perspectives from Christian thinking to such issues as city problems, community development, social injustice, racial integration and development, pluralism, and life-styles). Other subjects studied have been contemporary spirituality (contemplative and active), poverty, celibacy and obedience, Jesus people, communes, rat-race drop-outs, liturgy, meditation, intercession and the theology of Mark.

Suburban Christianity takes a beating in 'Nine Point Five Theses', couched in deliberately provocative terms for study groups. 'Weak churches must be shut down. The suburban church is not only a pain-killer but a gospel-killer. It avoids the real issues, harms people, prevents abundant living.'

I commented:

There are those, however, carrying on deeply effective ministries in suburban churches who have valid reasons for refusing to abandon all church buildings for a cellular structure. Modern man's needs include parish churches, liturgical worship in cathedrals hallowed by time, even the despised hymn-lesson sandwich.

I have quoted fairly fully, because in contrast to UTU's realistic, on-the-spot, ongoing approach, those much heralded commando campaigns, upon which so much hope was based and enthusiasm built up, seem to have been the merest scratching on the surface – an evasion of the real issues which remained untouched by those sporadic visits to factory canteens.

UTU was, even if it was not recognized as such, in a way a response to a plea made at a Free Church Federal Congress at Cardiff by Rev. Brian Duckworth, then a Methodist minister in that city.

He was leading a discussion on the theory and methods of evangelism, warmly commending a Scripture Union publication, *On the Other Side*, which was the report of the Evangelical Commission on Evangelism – although it came from the conservative-evangelical 'stable' to which he did not adhere. Mr Duckworth said:

> The image we have presented is that of a religious building. To shape a building deliberately like a church is not to invite people to come in but to identify the building with something they know is not for them, because they are not religious. Evangelism is but one activity within the total ministry. There are whole areas of contemporary life in which there is no shared experience across the frontiers of belief and unbelief. I believe we shall have to get away from mass evangelism which has not been justified in results or its enormous expenditure. It is our task to create the new outlook, understanding the world as it is, and offer it our gospel with all its secularity and opportunity.

This was very much in line with the 'religionless Christianity' then being so strongly espoused. It was (and is) a note needing to be sounded. But there has since been an increasing recognition that 'religionless' and 'secular' Christianity is not enough, and there has been a welcome reawakening of interest in meditative and contemplative prayer, especially as delineated in some of the writings of Thomas Merton (who was also very much a protagonist of incarnational Christianity and deeply concerned about social issues and practical peace-making). In inner city Sheffield, however, John Vincent stubbornly plugging away at his own line, continues to *do* by steady persistence what so many merely proclaim from comfortable suburban pulpits.

I have heard Donald Soper quote from the *New Statesman* words supportive of the Christian faith or approach, underlining the significance of this unlikely source for such commendation by adding, 'And this was the *New Statesman*, not the *Methodist Recorder*, or any other semi-religious publication.' This was a characteristic quip which got its laugh from the congregation, and was a comment I tend to accept as a compliment as meaning that the *Methodist Recorder* was not overtly pious.

But what shall we say of Methodist Conferences, Free Church Federal Council Congresses, British Council of Churches conferences, Local Preachers' Mutual Aid Association Aggregates or Wesleyan Deaconess Convocations? There was so much talk, so many resolutions about the burning issues of the day, so many debates, resolutions, amendments and counter-amendments. And they so quickly became dated and often irrelevant as world events rapidly overtook the eloquence and verbosity of yesterday. Nevertheless, they often gave the lie to the ill-informed criticism that the church *says* nothing about world and social affairs and *does* less.

More widely enjoyed by the average reader than any of these reports, I suspect, was the series of 'silly season' stories from holiday resorts. Producing these entailed going to a Sunday morning service at somewhere like Weston-super-Mare, briefly reporting the sermon and the worship, then button holing holidaymakers as they streamed out of the church. All too often the ones I wished to meet were hurrying back to their hotels and boarding houses, leaving me with local worthies whom I did not wish to interview. So I conceived the idea of spending a Saturday night at a Methodist Guild Holiday House or Methodist Holiday Hotel, enabling me to meet residents from all over the country. The popularity of the series was out of all proportion to its real worth, which struck me as minimal, and producing the stories was something of a chore. One Sunday morning at Weston-super-Mare, I came out of the service in a state approaching desperation. The service and the sermon had been impeccably 'correct' but wholly lacking in anything approaching the newsworthy. My sole hope lay in the visitors among the congregation. Most of these escaped me, and those who did not had nothing of interest to say. At last one fairly elderly couple let it fall casually that their daughter was present, was with the repertory company at the local theatre, and was currently appearing in *Hot and Cold in All Rooms* and *Is Your Honeymoon Really Necessary?* as the company's leading lady. I waited until she arrived and made certain her picture was taken with her parents. It had not occurred to them that this fact had any news value! Armed with this crumb of comfort, I wrote up an otherwise uninspired account.

Centred in Exeter and concentrating on the south west, I saw and wrote much about rural Methodism. What I found profoundly disturbing was the way in which (in spite of superficial changes in presentation and the slow growth of ecumenical consciousness) grass-roots Methodism seemed to have been marking time over the decades.

In the 1950s, the *Methodist Recorder* ran a feature with the general heading 'Is Methodism Making Headway in Rural England?' The second of these, which I wrote, carried the sub-heading 'Devonshire Likes Social Gatherings'.

Rural Methodism has been, in a sense, my milieu, both in my personal life and in my reporting. I can lay no claim to have studied this issue or gone into it in depth as I know has been the case at some of the conferences at Luton Industrial College. But much of what I then found remains basically true today.

I recalled a garden fête I had attended.

> From all over a widely scattered north Devon circuit farmers and their families had come to hear the fête opened by the wife of the local MP, to purchase a wide variety of goods, to join in the folk dancing, and to enter their babies in a competition.

I also recalled

> a circuit rally held in a large field on the northern slopes of Dartmoor one blazing August afternoon, with wasps buzzing round the little chapel packed to hear the Chairman of the District; the auction of calves, pigs, live and dead poultry, and farm gates. One is constantly coming across this strange contrast in Devonshire Methodism today – the large gatherings at fêtes and rallies, the almost empty chapel on a Sunday.
>
> The love of a rally, whatever form it takes or whatever its

objective, is a distinctive feature of Methodist life in these parts. It is hard to shake off the conviction that it is easier to arrange a 'social' than a specifically devotional meeting. Although the farmers turn up in full force to the circuit rally, they have been so concerned for years past in raising money for the trust and assessments as almost to have overlooked that their main task as Methodists is to evangelize the countryside. There is often no insuperable difficulty encountered in raising as much as £450 to renovate the chapel, instal electric light and erect a new roof. There is less frequently a corresponding readiness to win the 'outsider'. Rural Methodism, in short, seems primarily concerned with rural Methodists.

It would be wrong to infer that the Devonian's love of social gatherings is in itself to be deplored, even when viewed as an integral part of church life. Not only is it indicative of a deep and healthy desire for fellowship, but in one sense Devonshire Methodism could do with a great deal more of it. There are still those to be found horrified at anything so 'secular' as a garden fête, who enthusiastically welcome an evangelism of the most tub-thumping variety entirely unrelated to the social life of the modern countryside. It is not uncommon to find a small group of country chapels, financially flourishing, whose unflinching fundamentalism renders them unqualified to address themselves to the new type of agricultural worker that has arisen in the last fifteen to twenty years.

The attitude that the church's sole business is spiritual has, paradoxically, led to an absence of a policy of aggressive evangelism. The present-day young farmer, finding his chapel elders refusing to run youth clubs or social activities, will seek his fellowship in the Young Farmers' Club, with its public speaking competitions and other many-sided interests, while his wife will go to the Women's Institute. This has led to an acute shortage of younger local preachers, and the harassed superintendent minister finds that, in order to make his plan, he has to send out to these country places Seventh Day Adventists and Plymouth Brethren – or a type of Methodist local preacher whose technique and vocabulary is utterly alien to the young agriculturist. The town churches will not have them at any price.

It was about that time that Mrs Elsie Salmon, a Methodist minister's wife, came to this country from Africa to conduct a series of healing services. In this, she (and ministers in whose Methodist churches such services were held) were defying a Conference ruling that Methodist premises should not be used for this purpose. Dr Leslie Weatherhead, an authority on the Church's healing ministry in all its forms, whose book *Psychology, Religion and Healing* is an authoritative work on all non-medical (especially Christian) methods of healing, had explained with customary cogency and expertise what he saw as the dangers of such *public* ministrations.

In this, he was (I think) quite sound. But he was less so when he wrote to the *Recorder* complaining about the reports of the service in Chapel Street, Penzance, in defiance of Conference's prohibition. The editor, R. G. Burnett, replied politely that the report was completely objective, merely describing what had taken place without comment. I also went to her healing services at St Mary's Methodist Church, Truro, and the Plymouth Central Hall. This coverage was indicative of the intense interest these services were engendering.

Later, I called on some of the people to whom she had ministered in an attempt to make an objective and impartial inquiry into the results of her work. Some significant factors emerged. The first was the impossibility of a statistical inquiry into the percentage of physical healings. The second was that, despite the paucity of the evidence, there was sufficient to support the claim that some physical healings had taken place, and at that stage, were being maintained.

This was, in Archbishop William Temple's words, 'the ecumenical age'. Oxford swarmed with American delegates for the eighth Methodist Ecumenical Conference in 1951, with their plastic macs (a novelty then to most English eyes) and their hats similarly protected.

The *Recorder* sent Raymond Stringer and myself to cover

the ten-day proceedings, which we did very fully, phoning much of it through to Fleet Street. The appearance of the paper a day before its publication date with almost up-to-the-minute news greatly impressed the American visitors.

They were also highly appreciative of the lecture on the Wesleys by the ninety-seven-year old Dr J. Scott Lidgett, who had been elected President of the United Church of Methodism at the Albert Hall Uniting Conference in September 1932. But they were greatly alarmed when in the course of the lecture he collapsed and had to be carried into the church vestry on a chair by stewards. When Raymond Stringer, who was covering that session, came out, Dr W. E. Sangster (who had a keen news sense) said, 'Don't you wish he'd died, Mr Stringer?'

The next morning, Rev. Dr Harold Roberts reported to the conference that he had since visited Dr Lidgett, who was resting comfortably in hospital. When he told him of the Americans' concern that his magnificent lecture had had such a distressing effect, Dr Lidgett replied, 'I always say preaching is of no avail if it doesn't take something out of you.'

The conference was heavy going. It included a lecture by President Umphrey Lee of Texas on 'Methodism in Relation to Catholic Tradition' and sessions on 'Christianity and Totalitarianism', 'Francis Asbury', and 'Personality and the World Church'. But there were a few chances of snatched relaxation. The *Recorder* ran a Methodist Travellers' Service Room in New Inn Hall Street which, as well as train times and recommended places of interest, had details of theatre productions. The New Theatre that week had the Folies Bergères. The two young ladies in charge kept the advertisement under the counter, feeling that the picture it showed was somehow not in keeping with the nature of the conference. They may well have been right – yet the night I went, I discovered that I was far from being the only conference refugee. The next night, true to form, after reporting a session on the impact of biblical criticism, I saw Bing Crosby in the film *Here Comes the Groom*.

En route to Exeter when it was all over, I gave a lift as far as

Bristol to an American delegate. He showed less interest than I had expected in John Wesley's 'New Room' (Methodism's first chapel), but was thrilled to see Hanham Mount, Kingswood, where Wesley had, in the eighteenth century's quaint language, 'consented to be more vile'. 'Do you mean to say that Wesley actually stood where I'm standing now? Well, ain't that something? Ain't that really something?'

Jane Sheldon was the keen, experienced and conscientious reporter the *Recorder* took over from the *Christian World*. She and I covered the 1966 World Methodist Conference at Westminster Central Hall, with delegates from all over the world. Besides our concentrated reporting of the conference itself, we buttonholed some of the more striking personalities, notebooks at the ready, as they came in and out of sessions. Among these were Rev. Setareki Akeat Tuilovoni, MBE, in his Fijian skirted costume. It was said that at the 1947 ecumenical conference at Springfield, Massachusetts, the women were so fascinated by his curly hair that they all wanted to pass their fingers through it. He permitted this, if they would give him twenty-five cents for his work among youth.

John D. Yue of Kowloon, Hong Kong, I had already met in Westhill College, Birmingham, where I had had to call with a colleague during the period of the Christian Family Conference. There he had greeted us with that extreme courtesy which so often puts us to shame. He was a woollen merchant, who owned a large tailor's shop in Hong Kong and, so Kenneth Greet's secretary told me, most of the men delegates at Westhill bore his name inside their coats.

Rev. Robert Fisher of the Aurora Church, Ohio, said, 'While the World Methodist Conference has been helpful in some ways, I feel that it has had some shortcomings. It has limited both God and the Conference to race relations and the ecumenical movement. What about crime, capital punishment, morals, disarmament?

Of all the church union schemes, the Anglican–Methodist 'Conversations' lasted the longest, received the greatest reportage, gave the most employment to printers, and proved the most abortive.

Rev. Jimmy Butterworth, the founder of Methodism's London Clubland, told me once that when there were some extensions to their premises, a *Church Times* reporter came up to him and, notebook at the ready, asked him,

'What do you think of the Conversations?'

'I haven't time to go into that now,' said Jimmy, 'ask him.'

He pointed to a certain rugged character who (though not a church member and something of a rough diamond) was one of his most regular helpers.

'Excuse me, sir,' said the man from the *Church Times* to this individual, 'could you tell me what you think of the Conversations?' The man scratched his head, pondered the question for a few seconds, and said, 'Well, where I work, they're bloody spicy.'

Disappointed as I was over the failure of the Anglican-Methodist union scheme, and not in sympathy with the climate of the self-designated Voice of Methodism Association, I have had reluctantly to admit that the way forward now seems to be from the grass roots upward. Ultimately, organic union will surely be found to be the only durable arrangement although buildings shared between Christian denominations are now commonplace, and United Reformed/Methodist unions abound.

On 25 December 1965 I reported the first of these. 'Union from strength at Bridport – Methodists and Congregationalists vote for one church' ran the headline. It pre-dated the Congregational–Presbyterian union. I later reported the Presbyterian speeches and voting at Newcastle-upon-Tyne, and Jane Sheldon reported the Congregational counterpart at exactly the same time in London.

At Bridport, too, the two local denominations voted by large majorities to form a permanent union, and voting took place simultaneously and independently one Sunday afternoon. The initiative had come from the Congregationalists about two years before, but the closing of ranks was not dictated by economic necessity or lack of support. It has been a union of strength, not of weakness.

This was the pattern of many later fusions.

An occasional assignment was a campaign of the Order of Christian Witness, founded by Donald Soper. It was non-denominational but the majority of members were Methodists and, as might be expected, it tended to be left-wing and pacifist. Young men and women, showing great courage, would stand on a chair and propound their particular brand of applied Christianity. In the early days, they tended to ape (if unconsciously) the mannerisms and use the very phrases of 'Doctor' (as they invariably called him in the days before his peerage), though later they developed their own individualities.

Donald Soper's presidency of the Methodist Church in 1953 coincided with an OCW campaign in Exeter.

Never in the history of Exeter has the large Civic Hall, used for political meetings, dances and all-in wrestling, been filled to its utmost capacity for two consecutive nights. The first occasion was Monday 24 August, when over 1,500 church people attended a service conducted by the Chairman of the Exeter District, Rev. James K. Whitehead. The following evening, nearly 2,000 people packed into the large hall, many being accommodated on the stage behind the speaker. There was a long queue, and 200 people who failed to get in attended an open-air meeting conducted by campaigners. Extra chairs had to be brought into the Civic Hall from the nearby Providence Methodist Church. For some ninety minutes, the President answered from the floor of the house with his usual agility and ready wit questions dealing with such varying subjects as socialism, Dr Kinsey's book, and (inevitably) pacifism. There was a noticeable proportion of questioners evidently determined to test the orthodoxy of Dr Soper and the young campaigners whom he was representing. With one of these he dealt trenchantly.

> Asked if it would be better for those engaged in Christian witness to concentrate on the saving truths of the gospel and not 'the things of this world', the President began, 'It is arrogant rubbish, and I am not prepared to listen to it any more, when a well-dressed young man tells me we should have nothing to do with the things of this world. I take it that he has a ration book?' He ended: 'Now I love you, but I don't like you at the moment.'

Exeter's OCW campaign was typical of several I saw in action in many parts of the country – especially notable were the ones in Cardiff and Tonypandy. I wrote

> As might be expected of a movement founded by this year's President, open-air speaking has played a large part in their strategy. Most of this has been of a high quality, and it is perhaps the OCW's chief significance that large numbers of young Christians of several denominations are being trained in this exacting art. There have been no highly emotional appeals, no open-air collections, and no 'bronchial harmoniums'. Instead, the Christian case, and its relevance to the contemporary situation, has been forcefully and intelligently presented. Many of these youthful campaigners have been speaking in the open air for the first time from some of the remaining Exeter bomb sites; and it takes no little courage (to quote an incident I observed) for a girl, standing on a chair, to continue witnessing despite the abuse hurled at her by a passer-by who, to the campaigners' regret, did not stop to argue. But I have seen them draw fair-sized crowds and deal effectively with questions and heckling.
>
> At Exeter City Prison, a mixed team, before about 300 male prisoners answered a variety of questions which included 'Who is Azrael?' They have visited the city's steam laundry and Fire Brigade, and revived a lapsed branch of the Post Office Workers' Christian Association. They have made contacts at every level of industry.
>
> Sometimes they have spoken to workers during canteen hours; but at a large ironmonger's they addressed them as

they took their afternoon break between piles of merchandise. They have visited a rag-and-bone merchant's store, hospitals, an open prison camp, a youth hostel, the YMCA, a cement works, the cattle market, and a brewery. They have concentrated on housing estates; and at one of these a resolution was passed by residents, asking the Free Church Federal Council to do all they could to see that a church (preferably a United Free Church) was established as soon as possible. They have held regular lunch-hour services, house-parties, and brains trusts.

From 1953 to 1954, Donald Soper was in the news far more than any of his presidential predecessors had been. Years afterwards, he continued to be besieged by the press for Christian comment on current affairs, and continued to be described as the President of the Methodist Church long after his year of office had ended. In 1954, he was constantly in hot water for answers made to questions addressed to him in the open and the *Methodist Recorder* somewhat primly reprimanded him for criticizing the Duke of Edinburgh for his '*apparent* lack of concern for religious feeling in his determination to play polo on Sundays despite all protests' (in a *Daily Herald* article mainly praising the Duke for his many fine qualities). He was also taken to task for criticizing the Queen's attendance at race meetings, Billy Graham and MRA.

Letters attacking and defending him poured in to the Fleet Street office for many weeks. It was a lively year and I was glad when he visited Plymouth of the opportunity this gave me to write an article making it quite clear that in my book the President was, in the *1066 And All That* sense, 'a good thing'. He was in good form that bitterly cold January day. It snowed, and I was a little anxious about my return to Exeter.

Calling upon all Christian people to renounce war utterly, he declared that he would do away with the armed services. 'And leave this country wide open to attack?' someone called out. 'We are wide open to attack now,' he retorted. 'We are harbouring by agreement a large number of American bombers. These bombers, in the event of war, would be directed against the East. What these wicked Russians would do would be to try to stop them getting off the ground. In the event of another war, people in Lincoln would be in more danger than those in New York. The best defence, if one is talking of bombing, is not to fight.'

And he went on:

'I am a left-winger. Every Christian ought to be a left-winger. I do not mean that everybody should be a member of the Labour Party. In fact, I only wish the Labour Party was left-wing.'

The overall impression? Just this: that the President is using 'the fellowship of controversy' most effectively to commend the gospel. There was the note of urgency, the reasoned argument, the appeal for unstinted and uncompromising obedience to the gospel's demands. And the deeply devotional quality as the meeting drew to a close, which is characteristic of the most real and effective evangelism.

In the summer of 1957, the OCW's main campaign was held in the Rhondda Valley, where its support by churches of different denominations was regarded as a considerable achievement, a barometer of the desperate state of church life generally, according to the Methodist minister there. Tonypandy Central Hall, where George Thomas, former Speaker of the House of Commons, worshipped, had good congregations; ninety per cent were women.

The campaigners, some 150 of them from all parts of the country, lived in 'families' under the care of commandants, in Treherbert, Treorchy, Pentre, Tonypandy, and Penycraig. As on previous occasions, they gave up a week of their holiday to do so, in common with Dr Soper, who led the campaign. They slept in chapel schoolrooms; Dr Soper himself slept in the Tonypandy Central Hall vestry.

This year's campaign followed a familiar pattern, demonstrating, in Dr Soper's words. 'how deep-rooted are some of our practices. OCW has a spirit and temper of its own. It has that within it which endures and works.' There were visits to collieries, hospitals, public houses, factories, canteens, and open-air speaking. Dr Soper invariably drew and held the crowds, and answered questions. There was also much open-air speaking of high quality by young campaigners, standing on chairs at street corners and elsewhere. As usual, they conducted services in churches and chapels in the area on the Sunday.

All the 'families' met each morning at Tonypandy for 'general assembly', where the true spirit of OCW was seen at its best. The assembly on 20 August was enlivened by the visit of BBC technicians and cameramen. They filmed part of the proceedings for inclusion in the television programme *Rhondda Round-Up*, transmitted on 26 August.

I also saw the BBC team filming Dr Soper addressing miners leaving the Naval Colliery, Penygraig, and answering questions at a whist drive in the town's Old Library. The BBC men admitted they had been greatly impressed by the campaign, and had continued to discuss religion the following day.

I attended a 'Hit the Headlines' session at Libanus Baptist Church, Treherbert, and afterwards overheard Dr Soper, in discussion with some secular youth club boys (who were probably quite unaware of his identity). I accompanied a team to a factory canteen, where they covered much ground in a short space of time, and made friendly contact. I went to a youth 'squash' at the Judge's Hall, Tonypandy, with Teddy boys and girls rock 'n' rolling, and finally showing a somewhat noisy interest in 'Christianity on Trial'.

The report was headed 'Rhondda Situation is "Desperate"'. Yet a year before, Tonypandy Methodism had been claiming to have begun a new chapter with the reopening of the renovated Central Hall by George Thomas's mother, Mrs E. J. Davies. Her famous son was the first person I saw when I entered the hall half an hour before the official opening. He took me by the arm and said, 'Come and see our lovely new Hall.'

There was a packed public rally one evening, presided over by Dr John Gibbs of Penarth, which held for me the attraction of seeing and hearing Rev. Reginald J. Barker, of whom I had heard so much. He had come in 1924, remaining the minister for eleven years.

> It was during his notable ministry, when unemployment in the Rhondda was rife, that the Hall made its great social impact upon the community. It was under his leadership that the cheap meal service was started and a boot-repairing centre and a toy-making shop were formed, and thousands of wooden toys made. Men were housed in the manse garage repairing boots. It was during his time, too, that Community House (which still functions) was formed.
>
> In an arresting speech (in which he characteristically quoted with approval Father Huddleston, Turgenev and Bernard Shaw) he said, 'Far too many ministers in wireless services speak about sin instead of speaking about God. When we are hard up for a theme, we start criticizing. You can fill a whole speech with it. Most of the trouble in the world is due to wrong-headedness, and not to wrong-heartedness. Some people are outside the church, not because of the worst that is in them, but because of the best that is in them. I do not need to tell any Rhondda person that I am not a Communist. But it has become almost treasonable to say anything for them.

The charismatic movement did not really impinge upon my consciousness until my time with the *Methodist Recorder* was nearly ended. I have no quarrel with it, but it never made the least appeal to me. That it has benefitted many, as have the Billy Graham rallies, I have no doubt. Indeed, I have come across instances which prove their value to some. But I am quite certain that had I met either phenomenon before my own personal Christian commitment, I should have been scared away from the very faith they sought to propagate.

I only had one charismatic assignment, six years before I retired. I was covering the Wesley Deaconess Annual Convocation at Lytham St Annes, and had been asked to report during that period a charismatic conference at Pendlebury Methodist Church, Swinton. 'Anything may happen,' warned Rev. John Hully at its outset. What in fact did happen was not perhaps at first what the congregation of ardent evangelicals expected or indeed wanted. The afternoon began innocuously enough with some spontaneous praying and hymn singing. Two personable sisters, Lelie and Reka Molnar, sang gospel songs they had themselves composed with their own guitar accompaniment. There was a solo by a lady member of Tyldsley (Manchester) Independent Methodist Church, who was described as a 'faith evangelist'.

The surprise was supplied by that afternoon's main speaker, Dr John Pinnington. He was a member of the Russian Orthodox Church and a lecturer at the Bolton Institute of Technology. Expectantly, the congregation prepared themselves for some fervent evangelism. Dr Pinnington went to the lectern, and proceeded to read the catechetical address of St John Chrysostom which, he informed us, was read in every Orthodox Church on Easter Day. His erudite and excellent lecture was listened to in stunned silence. It was not so much that they disagreed – but was this what they had come to hear?

He said that the appearance of Orthodox charismatic prayer groups and their participation in interdenominational charismatic fellowships in the last few years was the most important thing that had happened so far in the movement. In the past, they had used two types of Christian worship – liturgical, formal and ritualistic on the one hand, free and extempore on the other. Each tended to assume that theirs was the only one that mattered and that the other was seriously defective.

His theme was that there must be a fusion between charismatic renewal and traditional churchmanship, and he insisted that the latter must recognize the spiritual value of a wholly predictable liturgy. At first, he said, charismatic worship tended to begin among evangelical Christians who had vague suspicions about formal worship. This was certainly true in the days of the great nineteenth-century revivals associated with the names of Moody and Sankey in this country. It was true of the Pentecostal movements in the United States and was also true of the very beginning of the more recent charismatic renewal. Generally speaking, it first began among evangelical Christians who inherited the dichotomy between formal and free worship.

A great many people drawn into charismatic renewal, whatever their denominational backgrounds, tended to regard what they found in their prayer groups as far and away the most important thing in their spiritual lives. Such an attitude tended to prevent fusion between the parish, the local congregation, and the prayer group. On the other hand, many came into charismatic renewal and had then grown to value and cherish the formal liturgies of their own churches. He said it was possible to value intensely the prayer and communion we had with God equally in charismatic groups and in the most elaborate liturgical forms of worship.

> We cannot afford to rest where we are at the moment and be content with the compromise by living our Christian lives on two planes that never intersect. Formal worship, as I find it, is a challenge to us to try to bring into a closer relationship the prayer of our charismatic fellowship and the churches, of whatever tradition.

This was, for me, delightfully unexpected, but perhaps for the congregation less delightfully so. There is a strange quirk in much modern journalism which invariably prefers the unexpected and (in the widest sense) the heretical. Rebellious utterances by a right-wing deviationist at a Trade Union meeting will be seized upon with alacrity by any self-respecting newspaper reporter.

Once at York, where the Aggregate of the Local Preachers'

Mutual Aid Association was taking place, a delegate criticized the movement's policy on the quite untenable ground that to get elected on its general committee (which had been, he said, a bourgeois one for far too long), one had to have gone to the right school and be a member of the Conservative Party. He also implied that there was something inherently undemocratic about its proceedings. He came nearer to being howled down than any speaker I had heard in my experience of many Aggregates, and there was at least one cry of 'Withdraw'.

Rebels at the Methodist Conference, the British Council of Churches, the Free Church Federal Congress, meetings of the Sacramental Fellowship, the Revival Fellowship, or anyone anywhere against the government, was virtually assured of space in our columns. At the sound of a dissenting voice, our pencils go into action immediately. It is a kind of second nature or reflex action.

On the one hand, I think the thing is overdone. On the other hand, I am a great believer in the gospel of the inappropriate. A congregation of intelligent Christian students of a radical nature could benefit from an address by a conservative evangelical saint such as Oswald Chambers was. Evangelicals have much to learn from radical theologians or controversial bishops.

Which brings me back to Dr Pinnington and that strange little charismatic conference. I glowed with satisfaction when, some time later I almost literally bumped into Mr Hully at one of Cliff College's annual spring rallies, and he told me that several people who had heard Dr Pinnington that day only fully understood what he was driving at when they read my report.

For all that, what I sensed was far more to their liking was the address given by the evening speaker – Dr Eldon Wilsdon, an itinerant Pentecostal evangelist from Washington, a pastor of churches in Texas, New York and Canada, who had been on a world tour, England being then his thirty-ninth country. He was a tremendously colourful, extrovert character, and his impassioned address was received with much hand clapping, raising of hands and stretching out of arms. There were spontaneous prayers, fervent hymn singing, cries of 'Amen' and 'Yes, Lord', and further duets with the guitar from the Molnar sisters. This was the stuff to give the troops, and perhaps it served its own purpose in confirming them in their accepted expression of faith. But it was Dr Pinnington's unexpectedness that I felt to be most useful, confirming me in my conviction that there is much to be said for being provocatively inappropriate on such occasions or at any rate totally unexpected.

Herein lay much of the appeal and power of Leo Sanders. At whatever meeting or occasion he was participating, he was capable of gently turning the whole thing upside down (to real spiritual purpose). It was most refreshing.

At Swinton, a specific time limit had been firmly promised by the chairman in view of the considerable distances to be travelled by many present. I was one of them – and as the appointed time was at last long overdue, I crept from my seat and (not altogether reluctantly) left them to their exuberance.

5 Interviews

I was never at ease while I was interviewing. When anyone, usually a Methodist minister, said to me, 'I'll sit back while you fire questions at me,' I was immediately struck dumb. In much the same way, I never really felt at home reporting Free Church Congresses, Local Preachers' Mutual Aid Aggregates, or Wesley Deaconess Convocations in churches – whether at a press table, in the choir seats, or in one of the pews. I felt rather as I would have done eating fried egg and bacon from the Communion table, and always welcomed the use of secular halls for such assemblies.

The easiest and most pleasant person to interview was Dr Maldwyn Edwards – one of Methodism's annually elected Presidents, an authority on the Wesley family, superintendent of Central Halls and, on a personal level, a refreshing acquaintance and friend. I first met him when he was a minister at Bristol Central Hall (pioneered by his father-in-law, Rev. John A. Broadbelt). During the war, he maintained a fearless ministry in the Old Market building, during the fiercest of the German blitz upon that city, often during Sunday worship. He was always a powerful, popular and highly individual preacher. After the war, I caught up with him again when he was speaking at the anniversary of Sheffield Victoria Hall.

I wrote,

> Dr Edwards, who has a gift for dispelling popular illusions, declared, 'After the last war, we supposed we should attain our dreams. So at Methodist rallies we still continued to sing "These things shall be: a loftier race" or Blake's New Jerusalem. But unemployment and economic depression led

to September 1939, and war on a scale to which we had not been accustomed.

'When that war was over, we might again at Methodist rallies have picked up our hymn-books and sung about the kingdom of God that lies ahead. But we have known disappointment and disillusionment. Even at a gathering like this we cannot sing as our fathers sang about the kingdom of God that lies at the summit. We cannot talk about the golden days that lie ahead, because we are the children of two world wars and economic depression. So, many good Methodists and other Christians cannot whip up the energies a third time; they cannot believe that even now, if we persevere, the kingdom of God will be attained.

'You are quite right to entertain that doubt, because it is surely wrong to believe that God has his favourites, and that we have to strive and suffer in order that at some hypothetical future date more favoured generations should enjoy the favour of God. It is a travesty of his character and a denial of his nature. Jesus said the kingdom of God had come already. The laws of God are in operation all the time. We have to realize and accept them.'

I was still reporting his pulpit utterances and manner when he had become Warden of the New Room, Bristol in 1972 (an appropriate appointment, if ever there was one).

It is said that men grow to resemble that which they love; and to see Dr Maldwyn Edwards preaching in the New Room, Bristol, is to be reminded irresistibly of John Wesley. There was a small but exceedingly attentive congregation for a sort of pre-Advent service on a recent November afternoon. It is difficult not to fidget in those straight-backed pews, and impossible to do so when Dr Edwards is the preacher, from the moment when he removes his glasses, throws back his leonine head, and fixes one with his blue hypnotic eyes. He has no notes, of course and at times, as he flings out his arms in an expressive gesture and throws his head heavenward, one suspects that he is entirely oblivious of his surroundings or of any other human presence – until, about two-thirds of the way through, he looks down from the high pulpit, opens his eyes still wider, and exclaims (quite needlessly) 'And now ... if you're still with me'.

A few paragraphs later on I observed:

No one I know has a greater zest for life than Dr Edwards. When he was President of the Conference, he once said to me, 'I'm enjoying every hour of every day, every minute of every hour, and every second of every minute.'

There was an endearing simplicity about this man of wide learning who made such a lasting contribution to the history of the Methodist people and especially of the Wesley family. I called on him once in his Cardiff manse (when he was Chairman of Methodism's Cardiff and Swansea District) in Mrs Edwards's absence. Abruptly, as if in a sudden recollection, he said, 'My wife said I was to give you biscuits and coffee.' He brought in the biscuit tin in bachelor fashion, then disappeared again into the kitchen. After a few minutes, his voice came plaintively, 'Douglas, do you think this is all right? I'm not sure I've done it correctly.' He came in with a steaming cup of ground coffee. The coffee grains were floating on top of the milk. I sipped it. At least it was piping hot.

'Well?' he said.

'It's very nice,' I said politely.

'Well, let us not exaggerate, Douglas,' said Dr Edwards, unconsciously adding to our stock of family sayings.

When in 1957 I interviewed him about his recent visits to Junaluska World Methodist Council, to the Emory University at Atlanta, Georgia (as a visiting Professor of Theology), to India, Ceylon (as it was then), and New Zealand, he asked me how many words I wanted, and dictated as he paced his study. Almost all I had to do afterwards was to type the interview straight from my shorthand notebook – in contrast to the sorting out and rearranging of material necessary in every other case. The length was right to within ten words or so.

I learned one trick from television interviewers; it was an elementary one and I adopted it in a milder, kinder form. This was simply to say, after a vague generalization had been made, 'In what way?' A minister might say, 'This church is spiritually strong.' Asked to specify *how* in precise terms, he would sometimes become strangely silent.

My first post-war interview was with Dr Francis Westbrook, concerning the revived Methodist Church Music Society. Commenting on the innate conservatism of most congregations, he said, 'Why must we so persistently cling to such old favourites as "Lydia" and "Wilton" (quite good tunes, of course), and completely ignore the "Old 113th", a great favourite of Wesley? We desperately need a greater breadth and catholicity.'

Dr W. Lawson Jones was then at Leeds, engaged on (to quote the headings) 'Psychological Work as a Method of Evangelism: Help to Servicemen on Returning to Civilian Life'. My report began:

> Under the ministry of Rev. W. Lawson Jones MA, the work of psychological healing begun at Brunswick Church, Leeds, by Rev. Leslie D. Weatherhead, who established a clinic in 1925, is being carried on and extended. During the past three years (1943–6) many people have come to him for treatment; the church secretary makes appointments for people from all over the world.

My interview with Dr Russell Maltby at Ilkley (where he had been Warden of the Wesley Deaconess College) appeared on his eightieth birthday. One of Methodism's great names, he was at that age looking forward, and I had some difficulty in persuading him to reminisce. He skipped over the past; then his eyes lit up, and he said, 'I took a hand in starting the Ilkley Council of Christian Citizenship. We began a series of monthly letters, which we have kept going, with a scheme of distribution worked out for them.' He listed their names: Canon Cockin of St Paul's, Rev. Frederic Greeves, Dorothy Sayers, the Bishop of Lichfield, the Very Rev. John

C. Tiarks (Vicar of Bradford and Provost of the Cathedral Church), Leslie Weatherhead, the Bishop of Bradford, Professor Norman Snaith, Professor T. E. Jessop, and Mervyn Stockwood. He was still preaching. 'I have been in Ilkley too long to preach old sermons, of course, so it means a new one each time ... I have always been a rebel, and am still unrepentant. Rebels are very necessary, and there is a shortage of them just now.'

Rev. William Potts spoke enthusiastically about a daring experiment in prison. He was chaplain to Wakefield's training prison, where the New Hall Camp was then a daring experiment in penal administration. It was opened in 1936 and, the first of its kind in the country, it was designed for first offenders. Mr Potts said that over eighty per cent of the men who came there never again went to any prison, 'which is a very astonishing figure'.

In 1947 the Vice-President of the Methodist Conference was R. J. Soper, a Barnsley-based timber merchant. He was a friendly, bouncy little man to whom I instinctively warmed. He forecast a great year for Methodism, rejoicing in lively churches he had visited, but warned: 'Do not measure by noise and bustle. Activity is not always a sign of progress. There is ceaseless activity on a treadmill, but not an appreciable amount of noise.'

Mr T. B. Heath was Probation Officer for Derbyshire. He was an evangelical Anglican, whose passionate plea was for youth clubs for the under-fourteens, a largely neglected age group. 'There must be,' he said, 'a very much broader outlook on the part of those responsible. Things will happen in their church halls which will shock them if they get these boys in. At present, church facilities are normally confined to the children of church members, and I know of churches where membership of a youth club is dependent upon coming to church once a week. That is approaching the problem from the wrong end ... I should like to see street corner clubs such as I had to do with in London. The youngsters smashed everything in the place for the first few weeks. They have got to get that out of their systems first.'

This made an instant appeal to F. D. Wiseman, who wired at once for the man's picture. His slightly bemused, not to say startled, picture accompanied the interview in the issue of 30 January 1937 headed 'Youth Clubs are Needed for the Under-Fourteens'. Perhaps they still are.

Factory visitation was beginning. In February 1947 I reported:

> Ever since 1944 something new in evangelism has been carried out in Leeds by Rev. G. Douglas Moralee on behalf of the Holbeck branch of the Leeds Methodist Mission. Taking the form of pastoral visitation to the factories, it is a method of presenting the gospel which might well commend itself to ministers in towns where commando campaigns have been held.

It was a full-scale interview, even by 1947 standards, and 'something new' was not really quite true. But the minister who grumbled to me that this was something many of them had been doing for years, and who demanded to know why all this space should be given for the young Douglas Moralee, was one of many instances I came across of that professional jealousy which is one of the constitutional hazards of the ministry. By and large, I have gained over my years of religious journalism a great respect for the average, unsung Methodist minister. But many experiences of pettiness, jealousy, and sheer bloody-mindedness produce a corroding cynicism – and had I not had my own Christian experience and convictions before embarking on the long journey of church reporting, so much more hazardous to religious faith than secular journalism, I should very quickly have become impregnable against all that the most persuasive Christian apologists could say, and have been virtually conversion-proof.

That is one reason why full-time reporters on a Methodist paper should be convinced Christians, if not Methodists. The *Recorder* has never been less denominationally insular than today. But the obvious advantage of reporters being Methodists is their ability to comprehend the ethos of Methodism.

Yet somehow one has to combine this with an objective, impartial approach. This is damnably difficult, perhaps impossible. On the whole, I think I failed. But by God, I did try.

Of all the many and varied interviews I wrote, the one I recall with the greatest degree of nostalgic affection is that headed 'Portrait of a Seafarer'. Skipper Ernest Pine was, in 1952, in his eighty-first year. He was a little man with a weather-beaten face. He began his colourful sea career at the age of twelve, fishing in the North Sea. He retired in 1922, and was a regular worshipper at Falmouth's Central (earlier Wesley) Church. He was in the West Indies in 1901 when the Martinique eruption took place. After two or three years he returned home and worked for two summers in the Brynhild, which won the King's Cup in 1902 and 1904. His eyes twinkled as he said, 'We had supper with King Edward at Cowes. We were a bit swanky then.' He sailed to many strange lands and saw many strange sights. He visited all the West Indian Islands, was in Ireland for six years as skipper of the Excelsior, and skipper of the Shira built in Loch Fyne and christened by Princess Louise.

He was a man of strong, simple faith. He was prone to cry out 'Hallelujah!' or 'Praise the Lord!' in church. Today I suppose he would be called a charismatic and his behaviour accepted in some measure, even by those (like myself) slightly embarrassed by it. But Central, Falmouth was traditional, respectable, and (as Skipper himself might have put it) 'a bit swanky'. His family rationed him to two such ejaculations per service. But one Sunday when the organist (whom of course he knew well personally) played a selection of Moody and Sankey hymns for the collection voluntary, Skipper was delighted and could not restrain himself. When the playing (and his singing I do not doubt) stopped, he called out, 'Good old Fred! That was lovely!'

He told me the story of his conversion. 'One day in 1896,' he said, 'I was in the Bristol Channel in a smack called the Pilgrim when there came one of the severest storms I have ever known on the Cornish coast. The third hand asked me if I would offer up a prayer. I had been brought up in a Methodist home in Brixham, and knew what it was to see "the family altar". I loosed my legs and arms from the wire tackling of the ship, and knelt down, but no words would come. I went back again, and made myself secure in safety in the wires and ropes. My colleague said, "Ernest, have you done it?" I replied, "No, we are too cowardly. We were brought up in God-fearing homes, and now that we are in danger we are trying to cry to God Almighty for mercy."

'Later the skipper asked me to pray. I knelt down again, and God put words into my mouth. Three weeks before, I had been to an evangelistic service, and the evangelists had sung "Jesus, Saviour, pilot me". As the big vessels were going away to the deep water, and the small ones to the shallow water, so the hymn came to me then. I knelt down in all the fury of that storm and sang, "Jesus, Saviour, pilot me". The scene was changed; my mate and I went away to safety; fear had left me, and I caught hold of the few ropes I thought were safe. I have been singing "Jesus, Saviour, pilot me" ever since.'

Later on he told someone: 'That young man sat down and talked to me, asked me questions, and as I talked to him he made funny little squiggles in his notebook. And when I got my *Methodist Recorder*, there it was, all I'd said to him.'

6 Acts of God

Floods, blizzards, national disasters, all had their 'religious' slant and impact upon Methodist life and worship. Methodism usually stands up well to such 'acts of God'. In the blizzard of 1947, services were held in villages isolated by snow. The Methodists weathered the storm and made the best of a bad situation.

Typical headlines were 'Homes, Churches Hit by the Floods', 'And Now the Mammoth Clean Up: West Country Takes Stock', 'Floods Swamp Half Britain: West Country Again Badly Affected', and 'West Country Pensioners Lose Home in Widespread Floods'. Later, floods hit Selby, Doncaster and York.

The two most disastrous national occurrences which came my way were the Lynmouth floods of 1952 and the collapse of the coal tip at Aberfan. The Welsh tragedy resulted in the deaths of many children, some of whom were members of the Methodist Sunday School. This was a story got by phone. However when, in the words of the headline, there were 'Heavy Methodist Losses in North Devon Disaster' with 'Life and Property Destroyed', in the words of the byline, making the most of *Recorder* involvement, I 'toured the stricken area'. In a council house occupied by seven Methodists, as disaster overwhelmed the household an attempt was made to get Mrs Floyd senior, an invalid, out of the house. This had nearly been achieved, when a tremendous gulf of water swept the house and all in it down the river. Mr Tom Floyd was the only one saved. Mr Fred Floyd could have saved his own life, but was lost trying to save the life of his mother. One house completely disappeared, but its occupants, a man and wife, their ten-year-old daughter and an eighteen-month-old child were saved, as if by a miracle. When about a week later I visited the devasted village again, descending the steep hill from Lynton with Rev. Palmer Morris in the van which was operating a shuttle service, I saw pneumatic drills and concrete mixers at work, workmen breaking up foundations as part of a scheme to turn the river back to its original course and construct new foundations for fresh buildings.

Methodists all over the country were foremost in financial and other forms of support. Rev. James Whitehead, then Chairman of the Exeter Methodist District, interrupted his holiday at Tenby when he heard of the disaster. When he left the day after taking part in the chapel service there, he found that folk had begun to lift up their heads again. A man said to him, 'Last weekend a wave of disaster hit us. Today a wave of love has hit us.' Offers of help poured in; some offered to accommodate tired mothers and children, or those deprived of their homes. Methodism's Relief Fund, always at the disposal of those affected by such tragedies, was able to contribute a sizeable sum from collections in Methodist churches throughout the west country. The newly-appointed headmistress of Barbrook Methodist Day School offered to accommodate two people in her house. She herself had been marooned in Barbrook, on the east side of the river, without light or water. I was able to report:

> no more parcels of clothes are required, so magnificent has been the response.

A year after this

> most severe river flood disaster ever known in the country,

I visited the picturesque village of Lynmouth and the neighbouring hamlet of Barbrook again, to find that through the generosity of Methodists who contributed a total of £13,767, every appeal for help had been met. The treasurer was the eighty-five-year-old Rev. J. Ash Parsons, who still motored to his preaching appointments.

Twenty-one years later, I went to Lynton again. It had long since been rebuilt; the four-year task had cost about £725,000. The river channels as carved out by the flood were accepted, and every measure was taken to ensure that the 1952 disaster could never be repeated – a disaster in which thirty-four people lost their lives on Exmoor, twenty-eight of them at Lynmouth itself. Some 93 houses and buildings and 6 bridges were swept away or so severely damaged that they had to be demolished and 132 vehicles were carried out to sea. In all 114,000 tons of debris were removed from the river channels, the estuary, and Lynmouth generally.

In October 1962, there was a tragic crash on the A38 between Bristol and Gloucester, when eleven members and friends (including the leader) of St Andrew's Methodist Church youth club, Filton, Bristol, were killed. The minibus in which they had been travelling collided with a parcels lorry. It was a tragedy that shocked the whole country and Methodism in particular.

They were on their way to Cheltenham for an evening arranged by the National Association of Youth Clubs. There the young people would have received awards in connection with the National Endeavour courses they had taken during the past two years. Their activities had included mountaineering, camping and canoeing. I succeeded in getting pictures of all but one of those who had been killed – as well as their minister, Rev. Sidney Fittall. The pictures showed keen-looking, smiling Christians, most of them young, although their ages ranged from 18 to 62. The leader was a man with a genius for work with young people, who never expected them to do anything he was not prepared to do himself. The 22-year-old assistant leader, whose parents were also killed, was described as 'keen on adventure and the open air life', and would have received a highly commended award at Cheltenham had they reached their destination safely. They were key members of a club which had been in existence for twenty years. It had twelve members and a waiting list. It was one of those stories which, like the Aberfan disaster, one would have preferred not to come one's way. But it did demonstrate the resilience of the local people connected with the families and the church, and did much to reinforce my own personal faith, in contrast with the many encounters which tended to foster an attitude of cynicism. When I called on Mr Fittall two days after the tragedy, he had already received about a hundred letters of sympathy, many from Methodist youth clubs as well as individuals from all over the British Isles.

Magnificently as the Christian spirit triumphed over these natural disasters and accidents, they should not really be described as 'acts of God'. The phrase should properly be reserved for God at work through mankind in traditional and innovative worship, personal contact, human caring, and the Christian infiltration into all areas of life.

Drama became an 'in thing' in the age of *Jesus Christ Superstar*, *Godspell* and *Joseph and His Amazing Technicolour Dream Coat*. There were many inferior imitators, as well as such deserved successes as *A Grain of Mustard Seed*. As drama critic, I received shoals of plays, ranging from traditional nativity plays to more bizarre offerings that attempted (with varying degrees of success) by stark modernity to demonstrate the 'relevance' (blessed word!) of incarnational Christianity.

More intriguing than any of these was the production of *Wesley: A Man Against His Age* by Jack Emery at Exeter's Northcott Theatre. Mr Emery's twelve-year research included reading John Wesley's *Journal* and sermons. Being the son of a Baptist minister, he had a keen insight into the ethos of Nonconformity.

Wesley's early spiritual struggles, his conversion, and impassioned preaching in pulpit and prison cell were set in the context of a coarse period of English history. The bawdiness of this was at times reminiscent of *The Beggar's Opera*. Apart from Wesley's, only one conversion took place on stage. This was a jail scene for the dramatic second-act curtain, with Wesley exorcizing a wretched devil-possessed girl. Many speeches were lifted straight from the *Journal*, with two quotations from his sermon on the use of money. It was historically accurate – except for some deliberate anachronisms. Undergraduates mocked the Holy Club by singing 'You cannot serve God and Mammon' to the tune of the Eton Boating Song, and 'Oh holy, holy, holy' to that of the Hokey Cokey. A deliciously evil-looking devil made his first appearance by leaping through a circus hoop and singing, 'Give me the moonlight, give me the girl, and leave John Wesley to me'. He then remained silent, watching with evident satisfaction John's abortive courtship of Grace Murray, his unsatisfactory marriage, and his whole uneasy relationships with women. Tony Church, an actor of distinction loaned at that time by the Royal Shakespeare Company to be the Exeter theatre's first director, had a commanding presence and, I thought, a slight facial resemblance to Methodism's founder. His performance was one of great sensitivity, restraint and power.

Bolton's Theatre Church (which I remembered as Astley Bridge Methodist Church) pioneered some exciting experiments, helping to give dreary old religious drama a new face as much as the more publicized *Jesus Christ Superstar* and was as deserving as some West End productions. Leslie Marsh, its minister in those days, wrote and appeared in his own play *John*, which was more orthodox than Emery's play. He followed it up with *Francis*, a musical about Francis of Assisi, for which he wrote both music and lyrics and directed it. He also acted as commentator, in the person of Brother Celano (though here he was understudying). In Franciscan habit, he darted on and off the stage, imparting background information in a confidential, bird-like manner. The actor who played Francis, Patrick Smith, was the son of a rector of Bury, and

> exactly captured the devil-may-care impetuosity of Francis Bernadone as he leapt down to flirt with the gaily-clad girls. This sequence should, perhaps, have been twice as long. The audience needed to be more fully acquainted with the character of the gay knight-errant before he abandoned the pleasures of this world for the austerities and richer rewards

of a dedicated life. But Mr Marsh is nothing if not a propagandist (in the best sense of the word), and was doubtless impatient to answer in the affirmative the rhetorical questions in his programme notes.

These in fact indicated his Moral Re-Armament background. Or should the word be foreground? He had also written and produced *Joan*, in which he demonstrated that Shaw had not necessarily exhausted the dramatic possibilities of the Maid of Orleans.

In the 1970s, the issues of pornography and explicit sex occupied much of the church's time and attention. Speaking at the 1971 autumn meeting of the Free Church Federal Council in Bloomsbury, Dr Kenneth Greet, then Secretary of the Methodist Conference, praised the Festival of Light for its aims and objectives. Characteristically, however, he went on to say that almost any statement made about the so-called permissive society was bound to be wrong, because it was a mixture of good and bad. In many respects 'permissive society' was a misnomer, because there were many things that were no longer permitted, such as allowing people to starve. Participants in the Festival of Light did not dislike pornography because it was about sex, for sex was a fit and proper subject to be discussed in any Christian gathering. They were not against it because sex was not fun – for sex was fun, as he believed the good Lord intended it to be. Its sheer entertainment value had been a box-office draw from the time of Shakespeare up to 'the utter rubbish of Mr Kenneth Tynan'. They were against pornography, he said, because it divorced sex from responsibility and projected the whole subject into a realm of fantasy unrelated to the real facts of human love. Pornography and unintelligent attacks upon it now seem remote and unimportant targets in view of the nuclear threat, to which Dr Greet is now devoting so much expert and dedicated attention.

The previous year, Malcolm Muggeridge, as had always been his wont, brought to life a meeting that otherwise might well have been unremarkable. He was one of a panel at Carrs Lane (then Congregational) Church Centre in Birmingham to support a protest against the opening of a sex supermarket in the city. Or so he had thought. But what he found himself taking part in was a discussion of the attitudes and actions to be adopted. In the panel's muted approach he saw a reason for the steady emptying of the churches. 'As one accustomed to wrestling with the ministerial mind,' he confessed he should have known better, 'in view of the fact that the panel included a psychiatrist and two clergymen.'

This was all lovely stuff, and I immensely enjoyed witnessing and reporting it. Moreover, Mary Whitehouse was in the audience and Mr Muggeridge flew to her defence and to the side of the one member of the panel with whom he felt himself in full sympathy. This was the first speaker, Mrs Norah Hinks, a well-known Birmingham Liberal councillor, who had been leading the campaign opposing the sex supermarket. Subsequent speakers were, perhaps, too broad-minded for Muggeridge, who

> was at the top of his form. He fulminated with all the force of his considerable and colourful vocabulary, he went red in the face, he gesticulated, he pointed an accusing finger, he waved clenched fists. 'Since sides have emerged,' he declared, 'I must say that I am a hundred per cent with Mrs Hinks. I find it deeply abhorrent to whatever remains of Christian morality in our society that the instruments and stimulations of sick sexuality should be offered on sale like any other merchandise.' The most effective promoters of this, he considered, were the psychiatrists. He called for protest demonstrations to be carried out in Birmingham, with marches and banners waving.

Was this (already long forgotten) gathering an act of God or even an act *for* God? I do not doubt the complete sincerity of any speaker, and it may have been a source of enlightenment to some. But even this I doubt; people tend to depart from such debates with their own preconceived beliefs more firmly entrenched than before. I think its chief value was that of sheer entertainment, provided by its salvation from a somewhat boring meeting (despite some fine, sound and sane speaking) by the participation of a consummate master of the spoken, as of the written, word.

7 Embarrassments

It is not the great debates I remember when I look back upon Methodist Conferences. Rather it is the team fellowship always produced at the press table just below the platform, the pressures, the mounting tiredness and the sudden relief when I realized it was nearly all over for another year.

'We've broken its back,' Rev. George Luty, a regular, would say, 'and tomorrow we'll wring its neck.'

I gained a certain reputation, in the words of Rev. Edward Rogers, for being a person to whom things happened. I did, indeed, seem to be accident-prone. One year I was not originally assigned to the Methodist Conference held at Preston, but when a minister was unexpectedly prevented from attending, I took his hotel reservation. It was on the outskirts of the town and I was not greatly impressed; the proprietress, a blonde woman of ample proportions, said I would need a main door key if I wanted to return after midnight. I drove hurriedly into the town, and after some difficulty I found a parking space (one of many there that resembled the bomb sites that scarred the country after the war). Then carrying my ancient Corona typewriter and briefcase, I half-ran in sweltering heat to the conference hall. At the end of that first day's proceedings, our team were at last the sole occupants of the premises (except for a cleaner), and when (in the *Recorder*'s room) our typewriters had ceased clacking, the silence as Eric Pigott edited our copy was oppressive.

'I'll bring the car round,' I said, 'to save time.'

'I'll come with you,' said Jane Sheldon, seizing this chance to escape.

But I could not remember exactly where I had left the car, and the sites were widely separated. In desperation, I hired a taxi. Seeing two young conference representatives, recognizable by their scrutineers' badges, I called out

'Is there a car park somewhere near?'

'Why, if you've got a taxi, do you want a car park?' they not unreasonably asked.

At last we found the car park; but when we returned to the hall, there was no one there except the cleaning lady, who found us very much in the way as we came and went several times to see if Eric Pigott and Leslie Timmins had come back after (perhaps) a meal in the town.

We went to the railway station.

'Have you seen two men with briefcases come through these gates recently?' I inanely asked.

'Several hundred,' said the porter.

We thought it possible that they had by then caught the train to Southport where they (and Jane) were staying for the conference period.

We decided to go to my hotel to phone the Southport hotel, warn the proprietress of my possible late return and ask for a key. From there we phoned Southport, but they had not arrived. I obtained a key from the keenly observant lady of the establishment, and drove Jane to Southport where we found the anxious duo.

On the Sunday, we escaped from Preston by car into the country. Late that night in bed, loud voices in the hotel disturbed me. I pulled the bedclothes over my head, and eventually was just dropping off, when I heard the strident strains of 'Happy birthday to you!'

I sat bolt upright and looked at my watch. It was the early hours. I assumed that other guests were responsible. I got out of bed, pulled on my dressing gown, and crept outside, only to find the noise was coming from the proprietors' private quarters. I nipped downstairs, pressed the house bell, and, barefooted, went halfway up the stairs. The landlady – it somehow seems the more fitting word – appeared, and asked what was wrong.

I told her, with unaccustomed vigour. I do not easily complain. I am not one of those who summon head waiters in hotels when the food is badly cooked or lukewarm. I normally suffer in silence and I was not at ease in this situation. But the thing had gone too far, I could not draw back. I said the noise had made sleep impossible.

'Then it shall stop, if it's keeping you awake,' said the lady, who had clearly been toasting someone's birthday from the stroke of midnight for some considerable time. Then she added:

'They're friends of ours, gradely Lancashire folk who come here every weekend.'

'They may be gradely,' I said, 'but if I thought they were coming again this week, I should have to leave.' Then I realized I had virtually committed myself.

'I think I shall leave anyhow in the morning,' I said.

'I knew this would happen,' she said.

'Then you must be psychic,' I said. 'As far as I'm concerned, if I'd had an undisturbed night, I'd have stayed on.'

'Oh, don't try to kid me, Mr Cock, and don't try to kid yourself. I knew this would happen from the moment you came in that first night with – with your lady.' Warming to her subject, she continued

'It wasn't your reservation in the first place, was it, but a reverend gentleman's. I love my Lord, Mr Cock, as much as you do, probably more than you do.'

This outburst, perfectly true for all I knew, took me aback, and I replied that I was not aware that our respective affections for the Almighty were in question. I checked out the next morning, and soon found good accommodation in a hotel patronized by some Epworth Press representatives and my former Manchester colleague, Reuben Rees.

I had a slightly embarrassing moment at Wolverhampton when the Wesley Deaconess Convocation was being held there. I had been a fairly frequent recorder of these annual conferences, so that I was known at least by sight to most members of the Order. Motoring back to my hotel one evening after a series of public meetings in the area's Methodist Churches, I spotted two girls in the familiar uniform of navy blue with wide white collars waiting at a bus stop. I did not recognize them, but was relatively confident they would recognize me. It was a miserable night, and I thought it would be an act of Christian kindness to offer them a lift to the hosts and hostesses who had given them hospitality as is the Methodist custom on such occasions. I pulled up, and offered them a lift. To my surprise, they demurred. But surely, I said, they knew who I was. They shook their heads. I explained I was Douglas Cock, of the *Methodist Recorder*.

'Never heard of you,' they said.

'But you're Wesley Deaconesses, aren't you?' I asked.

'No, we're nurses,' they said.

Two men were also waiting for a bus, and though not actually accompanying the nurses, were by this time giving me decidedly dirty looks. I thought discretion was the better part of valour and drove hastily off. I have a lurking suspicion that as soon as I had gone, they said, 'I've never heard that one before.'

Some time after that, the deaconesses' uniforms, which had been almost indistinguishable from those of district nurses, were most attractively redesigned by Hardy Amies.

I was put on the *Recorder* reporting team at short notice when the conference was at Bradford. Most of the hotels were booked up, and I made last minute reservation at a small private hotel in what had obviously once been a select neighbourhood. It was now less than a mile from a somewhat squalid area not far from what had a few years before been designated Yorkshire Ripper country.

A largely built, affable lady showed me to my bedroom, one of the smallest I have ever seen.

'Where,' I asked, looking around, 'is the wash basin?'

'There isn't one in this room,' she said, 'but there's one, and razor points on the landing.'

This indeed was the case. When I expressed doubts about the adequacy of this arrangement, she said that two nights later I could move into another room which had, she assured me, 'a sink'.

Downstairs, just inside the door, on the wall above the table with the visitors' book, where in some hotels one might see theatre offerings and church service times, was just the photograph of an attractive blonde girl, about twenty years old, with her name and the Bradford telephone number for use after 10pm. I checked out, and found an excellent small hotel three doors away.

Immediately after the 1967 Methodist Conference at Wolverhampton, I went straight to Hartley Victoria College, Manchester, for an Overseas Consultation. This was so well organized by the Department (as it was then more sensibly called, I don't care for the term 'Division'), who produced first-class reports of the previous day's proceedings each morning, that I felt it safe to skip one afternoon's session, confident my absence would not be noticed. I went into the city to see a film – what else? *Blow Up* was about photographic enlargements in crime detection, and was considered daring at the time, though tame in the extreme by today's standards. There was one lively scuffle in which two girls' garments were nearly removed. When I returned, I learned that my car, parked just outside the college entrance, was in the way of a group photograph. Locked, it had had to be *carried* out of the way. The entire conference knew I had played truant.

'Be sure your sins will find you out,' said college principal Dr Percy Scott.

8 The Authentic Voice of Cliff

Cliff College, a Methodist lay training centre in the Peak National Park, Derbyshire, offers a one-year certificate course in biblical and general studies. It is a unique and in some ways a strange institution. It was originally a large country house in the village of Calver some miles from Sheffield, owned by a God-fearing Congregationalist. It was acquired as a training centre for missionary evangelists by a certain Mr Guinness before becoming a Methodist college for the training of lay evangelists, in which capacity its first principal was Thomas Cook.

For many years it remained an ascetic, men-only institution. But in more recent years it has modified some of its strictures, turned its cell-like sleeping quarters into comfortable study bedrooms, broadened its theology a little (or at any rate tempered somewhat the exuberance I witnessed in 1939). Its history has been thoroughly recorded by Amos Cresswell, a former tutor, and President of the Methodist Conference from 1983 to 1984.

It is a curiously shaped building, with a domed tower, dining room, classrooms and the like, and has a terrace where large crowds gather on Spring Bank Holiday weekends for a sort of evangelistic jamboree. This is really my only association with the place.

I first went there in 1939, when my report was headed: 'Vast Crowds and Fervent Evangelism. New Hall Opened'. It took my breath away, and I found it almost embarrassingly hearty. This was the era before Rev. J. Edward Eagles and Rev. Thomas D. Meadley, two later principals, had somewhat modified the almost unrestrained exuberance I then found. It was a colourful, breath-taking introduction.

Monday is always known as 'the great day of the feast'; but it was not this which most clearly impressed me. Even before the mass meetings and the crowds of people who came in char-a-bancs and cars from all over England on Monday, I shall remember the intimate fellowship of the house party itself, the warm welcome I at once received, morning prayers quietly conducted by Gipsy Smith in the lovely little Chadwick Memorial Chapel, talking with the Principal (Rev. John A. Broadbelt) in his spacious and beautiful study, the spontaneous choruses that are sung at all times of the day, the communal living of the students, each being allotted his special task.

Staying in the house party and sleeping in a student's bedroom was that eccentric genius, Rev. G. Tinsley Peet, who had retired ten years before and who, until his death many years later, was a copious letter writer to the *Recorder*. The dining tables in those days stretched, institution-like, the length of the room. Meals then, as now, were preceded by the singing of the verse of a hymn; usually in those days it was a hymn of the type associated with the names of Moody and Sankey. Mr Broadbelt, an impressive figure of white-haired benevolence, having taken the measure of the eccentric guest, and having observed that he did not join in on these occasions, said at one meal,

'We'll sing that again for Mr Peet's benefit; I noticed he wasn't singing.'

'I'm sorry, Mr Principal,' said Mr Peet, 'I'm not conversant with these music hall ditties.'

He had come by train from Worthing to Sheffield, and complained to Mrs Maldwyn Edwards about the infrequency of the bus service from Sheffield to Calver.

'Somebody ought to tell old Broadbelt to do something about it,' he said to Mrs Edwards.

Her eyes twinkled.

'Perhaps somebody will, Mr Peet,' she replied. (Mrs Edwards was Mr Broadbelt's daughter.)

The speakers at the Cliff Whitsuntide festival (less than

three months before the outbreak of war) included such contemporary personalities as Rev. J. Baines Atkinson, Gipsy Smith, Rev. E. Benson Perkins, Rev. Joe Brice, Hugh Redwood, Rev. Charles Hulbert, Rev. R. James Day ('Happy Day'), Rev. W. H. Heap, Rev. Colin Roberts, Dr Martin Lloyd Jones, the President and Vice-President of the Methodist Conference (Rev. Dr William Wardle and Mr R. Parkinson Tomlinson), Dr T. Ferrier Hulme whose 'scholarly discourse was received with such rapt attention that even the familiar cries of "Amen" and "Hallelujah" were silenced', and such Cliff College veterans as H. H. Roberts and Herbert Silverwood.

There was a heat wave. The crowds poured in, arriving in cars, trains and coaches. I estimated that, at a conservative guess, they numbered ten thousand.

> As they thronged the corridors they were singing 'Let the beauty of Jesus be seen in me'. On the terrace they were singing 'From sinking sands he lifted me'. In the tent they were singing 'O happy day that fixed my choice'. Dr Wardle's assertion, 'How difficult it is in these beautiful surroundings to believe there is a crisis,' found an echo in many hearts.

Cliff College had another mammoth boost in a pre-war report, 'The Southport Convention: The Challenge of Radiant Christianity'. This I found, by comparison with Cliff College's weekend,

> more purely expository in character, not so spectacular. [Yet] both proclaim the same radiant gospel. Both are rooted in the same fundamental truths.

My report did not reveal it but I was not at ease there. Cliff and Southport (closely allied) were more fundamentalist in those days, with a degree of emotionalism and exuberance. One Cliff student staying at Southport for the convention was something of a rebel, a man more after my own heart than the others. One day (for the convention lasted the best part of a week) we played truant and went to the pictures; we saw a comedy starring the north country comedian Sidney Howard. Our cinema visit was frowned upon by some students who guessed where we had been. This was not the first time I had sloped off to the pictures. On my first evening there, I saw a French film and the film version of *The Mikado*.

After the war, I went to nine more of these weekend rallies at Cliff. I was accommodated in a student's bedroom as part of the house party, was always made welcome by successive principals, and formed some friendships there.

During my first pre-war visit to Cliff, I had met Gipsy Smith. In private conversation, I found him gentle, friendly and benign. His style of preaching and oratory would not, I fancy, now attract the vast crowds it did in his hey-day.

In those early, more expansive days – even before my time with the *Methodist Recorder* – circulation manager Reuben Rees had accompanied Gipsy on his tours. Harold Murray (a first-rate journalist of the old school) would report the meetings at great length. Mr Rees told me that once, when Gipsy Smith was in full spate in a packed Methodist church, he and HM (as Mr Murray invariably signed his colourful reports) were in an adjoining schoolroom. Gipsy was telling his life story, with liberal helpings of pathos and humour. The two men could not hear what Gipsy was saying, but could hear the congregation's reactions. 'In two and a half minutes,' said Murray, who had heard it all many times before, 'you will hear a loud laugh.' A slightly sceptical Reuben Rees looked closely at his watch. In precisely two and a half minutes, a loud laugh was heard reverberating through the church. Whatever one may feel or think about such oft-repeated precision and timing, this was clearly the performance of a consummate artist.

In *The Long Week-End*, a social survey of the years from 1918 to 1939 in Great Britain, by Robert Graves and Alan Hodge, there is a brief, accurate description of Gipsy Smith's platform manner when he was at the height of his popularity. The book has a chapter headed 'Art, Literature, and Religion', but Gipsy Smith makes his appearance in the chapter headed 'Amusements', along with such phenomena as the Shimmy and the Black Bottom, night club queen Mrs Mayrick, university students' high jinks, the Bright Young People, and Mah-Jong.

John Broadbelt was succeeded as principal by J. Edward Eagles, Thomas Meadley, Howard Belben and A. Skevington Wood in my time. During that period, there were certain modifications and a toning down of some of the overt enthusiasms and exuberances, while the occasions' rousing revivalism remained. In term time, I am certain, the atmosphere is much more low key; and the buildings are increasingly used as a conference centre for all sorts of Christian purposes.

In 1964, paying my first visit to Cliff for seventeen years, I found the anniversary retaining its freshness and making its own individual impact. Thomas Meadley assured me I would find much that was new and much that was still the same. There were, indeed, the same 'vast crowds' (a favourite Cliff cliché of mine), augmented by the youth camp which had by then become such a feature. The same evangelistic fervour was in evidence, the same appeals for decisions, the same responses.

That year's principal speaker was Rev. Daniel Niles, Principal of the Jaffna Theological College, Ceylon, and Secretary of the South East Asia Christian Council, who began his weekend theme of the pressure of God's advancing kingdom with an incisive and illuminating talk on 'An Asian looks at Church Unity'.

His approach and theme treatment undoubtedly disappointed many Cliff stalwarts and regulars. As ever, an almost split-second timetable had been presented to each speaker, stating precisely how long each should take and when the appeal should be made. Daniel Niles would have none of it. He conceded that his opening theme would have been more fitting at the end of the weekend. Yet he felt that it put the whole anniversary in its proper context, as that of a church which had inherited the Catholic and Puritan traditions. He said at the close of his talk that he was supposed to make an appeal. He declined to do so, convinced that this was more fittingly a time for reflection. 'We've usually had twenty or thirty responses by this time,' said one house party member to me, as we walked out of the lower marquee. Some of the official counsellors were particularly peeved.

On the Sunday morning, Dr Niles developed his theme with an exposition of the different meanings of the word 'witness'. At the close he said quietly, 'This is the place where an appeal is stipulated. If anyone wants to come forward, they can do so in the singing of the hymn.' One young man did so. (I noted that

> at the evangelists' service in the afternoon, conducted by Mr Norman Smith, twenty young men responded.)

But in the evening, after Dr Niles had spoken on 'the pressure of the invitation', he himself exerted none, and (I recorded)

> because of the nature of his message, he again rightly made no appeal.

On the Monday, as usual, cars, coaches and people poured in. What they heard were for the most part modifying utterances. That year's Conference President, Dr Frederic Greeves, declared that witnessing for Christ might include preaching; but there was no evidence that people three generations away from the church could be won by traditional methods of preaching. 'If they came here, they would not understand a word I have said, or the hymns we sing.' In the afternoon, a future Conference President, Rev. Kenneth Waights,

> in a characteristically forthright utterance

(in one of my characteristically journalistic clichés) said, 'Too many of us feel that Cliff is built for Cliff, Methodism for Methodists, the great Anglican Communion for Anglicans; but the body of Christ is for the sick, the fallen and the lost.

No unity, evangelism, conference, or Cliff College, can save Methodism, but only the spirit of God.'

At the same time, Bishop Reeves, at the youth rendezvous in the upper tent, was talking about the ministry of reconciliation between white and coloured races, adding, 'You must not take it for granted that because you call yourself Christian you are free from prejudice. There are many Christians in England, and I suspect many here today, who are up to the neck in prejudice.'

And the terrace meeting (for there are always a whole series of simultaneous happenings) ended with Dr Howard Williams saying, 'Don't be conservative. Don't try to live in the past. We are living in times when the church must not talk in "spiritual" terms.'

They lapped all this up. But it was clearly Daniel Niles who really got under the skin of some of the faithful, especially after his insistence, when expounding preachers' and students' most well known text – John 3.16 – that this was a social and not primarily a personal, individualistic text. My report ended:

> My most lasting memory will not be that of the vast crowds, but of a group of mainly young people standing around Dr Niles on the lawn outside the principal's house, pressing him to answer queries which had arisen in their minds as a result of his provocative and stimulating preaching, which had cut clean across many of their religious preconceptions.

A photograph showed Dr Niles emphasizing a point with a slightly accusing forefinger, faced by an aggressive young man in front of the little crowd.

The following year, though afraid I was already getting a little stale, I pressed on with

> Teenagers poured in to the camp on Saturday, and still more teenagers came on Monday. There were teenagers in coaches, minibuses and dormobiles, in saloon cars with religious slogans on their windscreens. There were learner

drivers with tigers in their tanks. There were teenagers in a wide variety of summery garb ranging from the sloppy to the slightly exotic. There were teenagers with transistors, long-haired, bearded youths, girls in jeans, Courting couples.

The principal (Dr Howard Belben) asked,
'Will the papers be as full of the young people here as if they had gone down to Brighton busting things up?'
'Quite,' I commented, 'but it all depends what paper you read.'
My visit that year was much enlivened by the company of Jimmy Butterworth, founder of London's Clubland, who turned up unexpectedly, and spent most of his time in my company. He was staying not at the College, but at a nearby hostelry. He was an old Cliff student, but had been expelled for smoking. Smoking is still forbidden there. Even on the Monday of the crowds, students will ask anyone seen smoking to desist. This is quite unenforceable, of course, on any large scale, and the ban is widely (if innocently) disregarded. I ended my report:

The image of Cliff is changing — slowly, inevitably; for the world is changing — rapidly. Cliff retains the warmth of its evangelism. It remains an extraordinary and unique institution that only Methodism could have produced. Last weekend was a heartening reassurance that it is not (as some unkind critics have said) the lunatic fringe of Methodism, but its evangelistic heartbeat.

I liked the last phrase so much that I used it again some years later at the end of a report. It came out as 'Methodism's evangelistic heartbreak'. Fortunately, the principal (Dr A. Skevington Wood) had a keen sense of humour and enjoyed the joke as much as anyone.
But it was my 1970 report that put the cat among the pigeons. The principal then was Howard Belben, a kind, friendly man, and I afterwards regretted that an unfortunate phrase somewhat embarrassed him.

Sunday afternoons on those occasions were always given over to the college evangelists, young men with a keen sense of mission. I decided that year to give the session a miss, principally because I wanted to call again on Crichton Porteous, whom I had interviewed before the war and had not seen since. When I returned, I found house party members enthusing about the evangelists' meeting and deploring my absence. Their attempts to tell me what had been said were utterly inadequate, and eventually one man lent me his tape recorder which he had used throughout. That evening I took a shorthand note from it with some care, ensuring a fully accurate report.

I went to town, as usual, in my report over such familiar figures as Tom Butler and Herbert Silverwood

(as ebullient and extrovert as ever). Above all, there was youth – in groups, pairing off, mini-skirted girls and long haired youths, some of them weirdly and wonderfully attired, laughing and singing.

Then came the unfortunate phrase, buttressed however by the cautious 'perhaps'.

But perhaps the authentic voice of Cliff was most clearly sounded by an evangelist on Sunday afternoon, before the coaches and crowds had arrived. He, ending the evangelists' meeting, began with an unrelieved sombre picture of contemporary Britain, continually punctuated with the cry, 'We're living in desperate days.' He cited the high divorce and illegitimacy rates, abortions, the permissive society, the Communist threat. In the face of all this, he saw the church as mainly 'spineless and powerless. It seems false prophets have joined the other side to undermine the foundations of the gospel.

'Here in Methodism we have no room for spiritual complacency when we are led by Methodist ministers who deny categorically the divinity of the son of God, the atoning blood of the Lord Jesus, and the resurrection. The only answer

> is divine intervention and an outpouring of God's spirit today.'
>
> Then a Billy Graham type of appeal. 'As we sing this hymn, you come, wherever you are, right out of your seats.' And about forty of them came forward, many of them teenagers from the youth camp.

I was wrong to have suggested this was 'the authentic voice of Cliff', and was mildly surprised at the number of letters that came to the paper, some critical of Cliff. In extenuation, it was some of the laymen most closely identified with Cliff who clearly thought it was, and who urged me to include this in my report.

Perhaps it was my next two paragraphs that more accurately defined the authentic voice, the essential ethos, of Cliff – like it or leave it. This is, quite simply, how the thing struck me.

> It is this uncomplicated diagnosis of a sinful world on the one hand, and a simple, evangelistic remedy on the other, that still predominates at Cliff. There is a modern beat to many of the songs, more than ever young people are attracted to this unique weekend; but the essential characteristics remain.
>
> There is no compromising accommodation with humanism or 'permissiveness'. There are no greys in the Cliff philosophy – only the blackness of a sinful world contrasting starkly with the whiteness of those washed in the blood of the Lamb.

9 Lay of The Last Opinion

When R. G. Burnett was asked, 'Who is Demos?' he always replied that the *nom de plume* for the writer of the long-running column headed 'Lay Opinion' covered a multitude of sinners.

He himself sometimes wrote the column. Leslie Timmins, in his tribute to Eric Pigott upon his retirement, reminded *Recorder* readers of the days when 'Lay Opinion' 'adorned the right-hand column written anonymously for almost a decade by the young man from the north of England who had taken up the editorship'.

There were others. Some were occasional freelance contributors, and at least one staff reporter was commissioned to write the column each week, come what may. This would have proved too daunting a task for me. But I was the last 'Demos', and for several years virtually the feature's sole writer. For the most part Eric Pigott, though sometimes suggesting a theme from some current church debate or concern, left me free to air my bitterest grievances or ride my favourite hobby horses.

It was a deliberately controversial feature, couched with the utmost provocation, though I always wrote it with complete sincerity. It produced some strong reactions, and letters not assigned to the correspondence columns were invariably forwarded to me.

> 'What do you mean by saying that to shout "Amazing love, how can it be, that Thou, my God, shouldst die for me" to the tune Sagina is the ultimate blasphemy?'

> 'Demos is at it again with his generalizations.'

'I don't know who you are, but you should be ashamed of yourself.'

One began:

'"Lay Opinion" on the Declaration on World Poverty is so untypically superficial I wondered if Demos is a syndicate,' and ended

'It is too late to wish you a happy Christmas, but I wish you a successful and nicely provocative New Year.'

Most were critical. Some were vituperative. A few were complimentary and appreciative. From the same correspondent came three letters.

9 September 1968:

'I do not consider your remarks concerning women's meetings at all helpful to the church.'

29 December 1973:

'I was appalled to read your article on 20 December and am surprised that the Methodist Recorder *is prepared to print such nonsense. If our circuit was ill advised enough to take notice of what you say some hundreds of people would be deprived of an evening service which they enjoy and value highly.'*

11 September 1974:

'I have written to you when I did not approve of your article. This time I am writing to say I approve wholeheartedly of your views expressed in the Methodist Recorder *of 5 September. I would not dream of calling a minister by his Christian name.'*

I praised the film version of James Joyce's *Ulysses* (which I had not seen), and was castigated, with some justification, by a correspondent who had, and who assured me it was boring. I did see it later, and found it lovely, deeply moving, and not marred in the least by its explicit sexual references, verbal rather than (as now tends to be the case) visual, nor even its occasional use of four-letter words.

Pornography was one of my pet obsessions. Basically, I was (and remain) anti-censorship, though I felt a little let down as a libertarian advocate by some of the more bizarre theatrical offerings. Videos of all kinds had not then hit the market.

The issue so occupied my consciousness for some time that one correspondent took me to task for 'jeering and carping at every Christian who protests at films, plays, books and acts which are not good, true, honest, lovely or of good report', and accused me of splitting hairs over the definition of the word pornography. Such counter-criticisms were all grist to the mill. I sailed in with a reply, which still seems to me sound, and perhaps of increasing importance when today's libertarianism is followed by the reaction of a counter-repressive puritanism (which may not be that far off). I wrote:

> Censorship is a notoriously thorny problem; but is rendered no easier of solution by a scarcely disguised philistinism. My own concern is that by and large it is not the pornographers proper who suffer. While merely erotic rubbish litters our bookstalls, we concentrate our fire on somewhat puritanical geniuses like D. H. Lawrence and James Joyce. It is an oversimplification of the issue to suppose one can determine what constitutes pornography by the frankness of the scenes described or the language used. Nor is it splitting hairs to insist that there is more than a delicate distinction between *Up the Junction* (presenting promiscuity in so sordid a light as to be almost a moral tract) and *Secrets of the Torture Chamber*, or between *Ulysses* and *Miss Otis Only Strips Twice*.

About that time, the British Council of Churches had brought out its working party report *Sex and Morality* and some members of the General Assembly of the Church of Scotland would not accept its Moral Welfare Committee's recommendation that the report be noted and welcomed for its 'reasoned and positive statement of Christian insight into personal relationships'. One parson went so far as to call it 'pernicious, wicked, and poisonous'.

As 'Demos' in 'Lay Opinion', I commented:

> Whatever the demerits of *Sex and Morality* – and more convincing speeches were made against it at the British Council of Churches, when it was presented at Lambeth Palace than some of the diatribes from north of the border – it was an honest attempt to deal with issues realistically.
>
> As one of the secretaries of Methodism's Christian Citizenship Department is known to have had a large share in its production (this was Rev. Kenneth Greet, then a secretary of the Department before it was infelicitously renamed the Division of Social Responsibility) it is perhaps neither inopportune nor unduly smug to rejoice that the Christian Citizenship Department is not the Mrs Grundy of Methodism. Its concerns range over a far wider field than Sex, Drink and Gambling – that trio with which the church has always maintained a strange love-hate relationship.
>
> In about equal proportions, the Christian Citizenship Department is accused of being too puritanical and too lax; this is the inevitable fate of anybody who has a sense of mission and whose feet are firmly on the ground. But holding up one's hands in pious horror or hurling abuse cuts no ice, butters no parsnips – and solves no problems.

I had in fact covered this BCC conference in the library of Lambeth Palace, presided over by Archbishop Michael Ramsay, who appeared to be half asleep as he afforded everyone carte blanche to speak for as long as they wished. Finally he summed up the matter in a masterly way that made it quite clear that he had not missed a single word.

A few 'Demos' extracts illustrate the extent of my obsession or concern.

31 July 1969:

> It is virtually certain that there will come – and perhaps a good deal sooner than most people anticipate – a reaction against all that has come to be known as the permissive society. It could be so violent as to usher in the opposite extreme, throwing us from the frying pan of libertinism into the fire of puritanism. It is surely the church's role at this

juncture to preserve some sort of steadying balance.

This may sound a tame sort of exercise; but it is to be preferred either to hailing the latest offering of the lunatic fringe as a masterpiece, or sending jeremiads to the press and our local MPs.

11 November 1971:

If only the recipients of the long awaited, hard fought-for freedom had proved their maturity by producing something genuinely adult, there would have been less call for a Festival of Light. The sincerity, intelligence and persuasive powers of the Mary Whitehouses and Malcolm Muggeridges should not be underrated; but the fear of a violent swing to excessive puritanism is a healthy one. Freedom is a heady wine, and one can only hope that the public, tiring (as it is already showing signs of doing) of acres of flesh on the wide screen, treble entendres on the small screen, and the almost routine explicit passages in new novels, will create a demand for something different.

Another strong concern of mine was the preservation of the *Book of Common Prayer* as it was before the philistines got their hands on it. It seemed to me then and it seems to me now that the incomparable prose of Cranmer and the hymns of Wesley and Watts were inalienably wed. The loss of such a possible combination was one of the reasons why I so deeply deplored the failure of the Anglican-Methodist scheme. 'You can't improve on Cranmer' became (and remains) for me an almost sacred principle. I returned to the theme again and again.

12 September 1968:

One of the treasures we share with the Anglicans is the *Book of Common Prayer*. A few, far too few, Methodist churches maintain a morning liturgical service. It is ironic that, when the Conference is broadcast or televized, protests are invariably forthcoming from those who indignantly inquire why we cannot have 'a traditional Methodist service'.

There is further irony in that, at a time when Anglican-Methodist union in the forseeable future is a distinct possibility, Anglicanism is currently engaged on liturgical reform. Perfection in this life is sufficiently rare to cause one to view with apprehension the revision of so consummate a work as Cranmer's. On this issue, I am not so much an old-fashioned Methodist as an old-fashioned Anglican. Which amounts to pretty much the same thing.

7 October 1971:

Liturgical reformers, happily engaged in substituting 'you' for 'thou' are living in cloud cuckoo land. My blood boils at the thought of anyone tinkering with the Lord's Prayer, the Creeds, the Gloria in Excelsis, the Sursum Corda, the Te Deum, and the Agnus Dei. I could more easily stomach the whole of Shakespeare being drafted in Scouse than one syllable of Cranmer being changed. A rising generation by no means devoid of a sense of beauty or a love of imagery will not be attracted to the church by any puny substitute for 'We have erred and strayed from Thy ways like lost sheep' or 'Thou sittest at the right hand of God in the glory of the Father'.

22 November 1979:

It would be an act of unforgivable philistinism if the King James version of the Bible or the *Book of Common Prayer* were ever allowed to fall into disuse ... It is now, perhaps, too late to revert to the exclusive use of the 1662 rite. But I tremble lest it be totally superseded, for I cannot conceive a better use of the English tongue to express such deeply spiritual yearnings and consolations ... Let us in the pulpit use J. B. Phillips and the *New English Bible* (sparingly) and jealously guard the Authorized Version. Let us pension off 'Lord of the dance'. But let us honour perfection when we have it. Cranmer's Prayer Book is a priceless treasure. It is only when modern liturgists play around with it that it becomes, in Pope's words, one of the 'toys of the age'.

Did my strictures about this and other issues make a pennyworth of difference? I doubt it – apart from some lively church debate here and there. But I am not too sanguine about anything more concrete than that.

I wrote once supporting the use in public worship of the Methodist Lectionary. In the issue of 20 September 1979 however, I confessed that there were instances when the choice, usually of the Old Testament lesson, baffled me.

> I find myself facing a congregation of five old ladies, including the organist – by no means an unusual situation. How inspired are they going to be to know that 'these be the names of the mighty men who David had: The Tachmonite that sat in the seat, chief among the captains; the same was Adino the Eznite: he lifted up his spear against eight hundred, whom he slew at one time'.
>
> Expectantly, they await some message of hope, sustenance and comfort from holy writ. Perhaps it will improve. They shift uneasily and re-settle themselves. The organist pretends to be looking for the next hymn, which in fact she has already found. The preacher goes on: 'And after him was Eleazar the son of Dodo the Ahohite, one of the three mighty men with David, when they defied the Philistines that were there gathered together to battle, and the men of Israel were gone away.'
>
> Yesterday's news on the media had been of extreme violence. 'O Sabbath rest by Galilee.' The preacher goes on: 'He arose and smote the Philistines until his hand was weary, and his hand clave unto the sword.' I refuse to read, out of context, at Sunday worship, stuff like that.

Almost incredibly, I did not make that example up. But it still crops up from time to time in the lectionary, which I almost invariably use when conducting public worship – and as regularly discard when it does.

Sometimes I wandered into theological observations where, as a mere scribbler and layman I was really out of my depth. Commenting on the Death of God and *Honest To God* debate, the 'Lay Opinion' of 4 May 1967 ended:

> The average man-in-the-pew is apt to become confused when he hears from the pulpit the half-digested utterances of the latest prophet of the New Theology. (This was the title of a once notorious volume by R. J. Campbell published in 1907 – much of which differs so little from contemporary outpourings that one wonders whether what is happening now is a forward move or a backward swing of the theological pendulum.)
>
> The liberality of a Canon Rhymes needs to be balanced by the puritanism of a Garth Lean, the demythologizers by the insistence of a Quintin Hogg that the historicity and supernaturalism of the gospel are all-important. (Bonhoeffer should be read alongside P. T. Forsyth, significantly still in print.)
>
> Doubt (even when 'honest', and in spite of Tennyson) is to be feared more than dogma. I eagerly await a new paperback from the Bishop of Woolwich entitled *But this I CAN believe!*

(The late John Robinson had at that time brought out a collection of pieces entitled *But that I Can't Believe!*)

For its last two or three appearances, the feature dropped its familiar heading (simply transferring the name 'Demos' in its place). The editor, Michael Taylor, understandably did not want to risk the columnist's sometimes wayward opinions being interpreted as the paper's official policy. Upon reflection, I am inclined to deplore anonymity for such a feature, and think a writer should nail his colours to the mast. I no longer wholly approve of a practice I inherited.

Did we achieve F. D. Wiseman's ambition of waking up the church through news? A little, perhaps. We did, I think, give it a salutary prodding from time to time. And there was, as there continues to be, faithful and (virtually always) accurate coverage of Methodist and other church activities in all their varied aspects.

It was a privilege to serve so long on the best of all Christian newspapers.